GOOD LIFE A Zen Precepts Retreat with Cheri Huber

Also on Cheri Huber's teaching

GOOD
LIFE

A Zen Precepts
Retreat
with
Cheri Huber

Edited by
Sara Jenkins

Present Perfect Books
Lake Junaluska, North Carolina

Library of Congress Catalog Card Number: 97-65802

Publisher's Cataloging-in-Publication
(Provided by Quality Books, Inc.)

Good life : a Zen precepts retreat with Cheri Huber / edited by
    Sara Jenkins.
        p. cm.
        ISBN 0-9630784-2-9

        1. Zen Buddhism. I. Jenkins, Sara. II. Huber, Cheri

    BQ9266.G66 1997   294.3'927
                                   QBI97-40372

The quotation from *The Golden Age of Zen* (copyright 1996 by
The Estate of John C. H. Wu) is used by permission of Doubleday,
a division of Bantam Doubleday Dell Publishing Group, Inc.

Insect illustrations by Uwe Bangert from *Das kleine Insektenbuch*,
Insel-Verlag, Frankfurt-am-Main, 1961, used by permission.

Present Perfect Books
Box 1212, Lake Junaluska, North Carolina 28745

. . . Not only the sudden perception of truth, but also an unexpected experience of spontaneous goodness, can liberate you from the shell of your little ego, and transport you from the stuffy realm of concepts and categories to the beyond. Whenever goodness flows unexpectedly from the inner self, uncontaminated by the ideas of duty and sanction, there is Zen.

John C. H. Wu, *The Golden Age of Zen*

CONTENTS

PREFACE

The people you will meet in this book are looking for answers. If you join this inquiry—if you look into these precepts as into a mirror that reveals ever-deeper layers of who you are—you will be embarking upon the journey of your life (literally).

Along the way, you will have the opportunity to learn from a Zen teacher who transforms life's difficulties into adventure. Cheri Huber addresses concerns raised by Zen students on this retreat—from anger and overeating and judging others to gossip and sexual behavior and lying to oneself—showing how to use those very aspects of our lives to win freedom from suffering.

Come with mind and heart open to discovering your own deepest knowing, and you will find that you share with your fellow travelers all that is human. You will savor the companionship of people whose taste for freedom enables them to patiently persist on this path. You will notice how they make small shifts in direction, from yearning for life to be easy toward learning to deal skillfully with whatever arises. And you will glimpse, at least, the understanding that you have everything necessary to find your own way.

The Buddhist precepts are guidelines for a good life. They vary in number and wording, depending on the culture and context for which they were intended. In the Zen tradition, the precepts can sound much like the Ten

Commandments. But the Buddhist precepts are not rules. They are more like signposts on the path that leads away from suffering and toward our own goodness.

The word "goodness" can suggest something very different from "a good life" (not to mention "*the* good life"). Fortunately, following the path of Buddhist meditation does not require one to become a "good" person first. Until I became seriously interested in Zen practice, I considered being good a means to an end; I was willing to try what I thought of as goodness if it helped my purpose, but what I really wanted was not to suffer. Buddhism, it turns out, is about precisely that—how to end suffering. Like meditation, working with the precepts can help us see exactly what it is that keeps us from experiencing the natural joy of being wholeheartedly who we are, of living this good life.

Each section in this book begins with the precept as it is given in the Daily Recollection which is recited in this tradition (page 132). That is followed by a four-part unfolding of the precept developed by one of Cheri's students, Arthur White, as part of his own preparation to accept the precepts as vows. I am grateful to him for illuminating the precepts in a way that I find encouraging, insightful, and thought-provoking, in language that points to the immediate concerns of our daily lives.

I am grateful also to the participants in this retreat for their willingness to share this experience, and, of course, to our beloved teacher.

Sara Jenkins

INTRODUCTION:
The precepts as a magnifying glass

The precepts are not rules of conduct by which we judge others or ourselves. Rather, they are reference points along the path of awakening—awakening to what causes suffering, what stands between us and the inherent goodness of life.

Thus, by "following the precepts" we mean incorporating these ideas into our awareness, developing the habit of examining our actions from this profoundly and radically moral (which is not to say conventional) point of view. With the first precept, for example, we consider everything in terms of harmlessness, not with intellectual analysis, but by simply paying attention to our experience, noticing what is sensed as harmful, what is sensed as harmless. That becomes a way of looking at life that helps us go deeper in learning what leads toward suffering and what leads away from suffering. Precepts are "laws" in the sense of natural law: this is how things are; if this, then that.

The discipline of following the precepts won't cause us to awaken—but neither will ignoring them. A more helpful attitude is to consider the precepts in terms of what is possible. The same is true in meditation: sitting still, straight, attentive, receptive, expresses a sense of possibility, honors a deeper truth of who we are. If nothing happens as a result of our sitting there, it doesn't matter, because we've already gotten so much just knowing the possibility of our own goodness. The precepts can work in our lives in the same way.

The precepts are about opening up to life. They address areas in which people tend to be closed down; we have a lot of childhood conditioning locked in us around stealing, sex, dishonesty, intoxication, judgment, greed, religion. As we use the precepts to explore these areas, we can see what our conditioning is, how it operates in us, how it causes us to suffer.

From this perspective, the precepts do not say that anything is not okay or that anything is okay. So, if not killing and not stealing and not lying and so on isn't the point, why bother with the precepts at all? Because there is something more important than having a rule and clinging to it because a rule allows us to believe we have figured out how to do the right thing. What the Buddha was getting at with the precepts, it would seem, is that we are unlikely to allow ourselves to be happy if we ignore these aspects of life. Another way of saying it is that the precepts support our inherent goodness against egocentricity. Killing, stealing, lying—all the things the precepts suggest avoiding—arise only from egocentricity, from the illusion of a separate self.

It can be very easy to keep a precept, depending on how we define it. Don't kill other people: okay, got that one. Don't steal large objects that belong to other people: okay, got that one. Don't lie unless I have to: okay, got that one. Don't criticize other people unless they truly deserve it: okay, got that one. No sex outside a committed relationship unless I just can't help myself: okay, got that one. Following the precepts will not make my life easier in the sense of being able to get away with things that require me to disregard my own inner wisdom, to abandon my heart. Rather, it can make my life more complicated because I have to pay attention all the time and look more deeply at everything that happens.

The Three Pure Precepts

The three pure precepts often are written, "Cease from evil, do only good, do good for others." In our tradition, the wording is somewhat more complex:

The precept of restraint and religious observances
The precept of obedience to all good laws
The precept to benefit all sentient beings

In retreats these are not addressed as directly as the "ten grave prohibitive" precepts are [see Daily Recollection, p. 132]. But the point of all of them is the same: to bring us into the present moment.

"Restraint" is part of our training to return our awareness to here and now. Just as a puppy, full of vitality, must be trained not to run out in front of cars, so do we train ourselves away from that which is harmful to us. When it's not diverted into harmful acts, all the joy and spontaneity of life can happen right here in this moment.

As for the "religious observances," each of us will discover the meaning of this in our own practice. For example, people on this path often become filled with gratitude and want to express that. In Buddhism, we can thank anything, since it's all the same. When we bring our hands together, symbolizing that your heart and my heart are one, and we bow, honoring that oneness, we bow to everything. That is another way of coming back to the present, to all that exists.

"Obedience to all good laws" reminds me of the commercial for kosher yogurt that says, "We answer to a higher authority." The laws of society are nothing compared to what we aim for in spiritual practice: we cannot be obligated to follow a law that is harmful. We must be free to take the responsibility of being in the moment, looking to our hearts, and seeing what feels as if it is in keeping with compassion. We are then obligated—and privileged—to follow the law of that goodness.

In the third pure precept, to "benefit" is to be present with, to not be separate from. St. Augustine says, "First love, and then do what you will." We say, "First *be* the compassion, then whatever follows will follow." Life lives itself, life lives me. My choices are to be with that experience or to believe myself separate from it. When I *am* that experience, there is no suffering; when I believe myself to be separate from it, there is suffering. So, it's really quite simple: being present or being somewhere else.

In my own mind and heart, I do not hear the word "sentient" in this precept. How would I draw a line between sentient and nonsentient? With everything I encounter, it hurts my heart not to be as kind as it is possible for me to be. Why would I not want to benefit *all* beings? Even "all beings" has an exclusive connotation—to me it is all Being.

Morality

It is essential that we not use the precepts against ourselves. If we approach them as things we shouldn't do, then when we do them anyway, we want to punish ourselves. That is abusing the precepts. To say, "I keep doing harmful things, I'm a bad person," is not helpful.

The heart of precepts practice is morality. This presents a paradox that we have to grapple with. Morality from the point of view of egocentric conditioning means that I have my beliefs about what is right and wrong and who is good and bad, and my job is to sit in judgment of myself and everyone else to make sure that I and they are moral. The morality of the precepts has nothing to do with conditioning. It is based in compassion and requires us to live completely in the moment.

But how to do that? We want a set of rules so we will know exactly how to proceed—but there are no rules for living that morality. There's nothing to write down. There's no way to know what to do in the next moment. There's no way to judge other people. For egocentricity, it is a dismal prospect indeed. But for the heart, it is liberation. Morality is the nonseparateness of the moment, and when our life is that, there is nothing harmful, nothing not given, nothing unchaste, nothing false, nothing wrong.

The best we can do is to keep bringing our attention back to the present, to our hearts, to what is right here in this moment. For short, we call this "coming back to here." Mostly, of course, we are "out there," which is short for being lost in egocentricity, our conditioned reactions, the ongoing dramas of who we think we are, and the suffering involved in that. If I try to figure things out from out there, it is never going to work. My actions will be my version of what is good; they may meet my standards, but they may not be good for anyone else, or even for me. We begin to see this in sitting meditation as we practice bringing our attention back to the breath, watching what arises in our minds, not assuming that we know, but constantly looking, seeing how we are conditioned, how egocentricity works.

Compassion

At this point, I never feel bad when I am aware of what people call "breaking" a precept. There's nothing to break. There's simply awareness that I have not been living in compassion, and I am deeply grateful for that awareness. The point is not to do it "right" and punish myself when I'm doing it wrong. That takes me further and further from the joy that is available right here. When we come back to whatever is happening when we are fully present, we *are* compassion. We don't have to try to *follow* the precepts; the instant we are at one with our hearts, we *are* the precepts.

For example, when I see a furry caterpillar making its way across an expanse of highway, with not much chance of getting to the other side, and I pick it up and carry it away from the road and put it on a tree, I love that. I love the tenderness I feel toward that creature, toward the life that it is, toward its innocence. There it is going along in life with no idea that it is on a highway with speeding cars—just like us: we go through life not knowing where we are in the big picture and whether a truck is barreling down on us and in a minute we'll be squashed flat. I project all of that onto the caterpillar; I see my life in that little creature. The tenderness I feel for it, I then feel for myself. And I can know that that tenderness is who I am.

That is, tenderness is another word for the compassion that informs all life. As I become more able to experience that tenderness inside me, I am more able to experience it outside me, and as I feel it more outside me, I feel it more inside me. I don't want to do anything to harm anything, because there's nothing that harms something else that doesn't harm me, and I don't want something as tender as myself to be harmed.

So, I don't want to use the precepts to punish myself. They are to help me be more kind, to help me live more in that compassion that is my true nature, to be in touch with the beauty and sweetness that is life. That's how I want people to experience the precepts—as a gentle, loving hand in the middle of your back that softly guides you through life, a mentoring loving-kindness that wants you to experience all the joy that life has to offer.

Discovering Goodness

What makes my job so easy is that when I'm asked a question like, is it stealing to use the office photocopier for your own stuff, or is it unchaste to fantasize about sex with somebody other than your partner, my answer is always the same: find out. Just watch closely, see for yourself what happens with an issue you're concerned about, rather than having a belief, basing a whole reality on that belief, and feeling limited by that belief.

I suppose an argument can be made from a Buddhist

perspective that I should make myself do or not do certain things in order to be a good person. But I don't think it's Buddhist, and, more important, I don't think it works. I ask you to consider how it actually might be selfish and egocentric for me to force myself to do the "good" thing in spite of what I really want. The result is that I will die having an image of myself as a very good deprived person, and as Ram Dass says, those uncooked seeds—the things I wanted to do but didn't—will simply sprout somewhere else. Why not have the courage to go through whatever it is as quickly as possible and get to the other side? Then it's clean, there's nothing left over, nothing to continue, whatever is there will be resolved. I ask you to explore this perspective within yourself and see if to you it has value, rather than assuming that as a spiritual teacher I've given it a lot of consideration and if it seems this way to me, it must be true.

Now, what happens if I am a very good deprived person? My belief system remains in control. I can be feeling really pleased with myself while leaving a trail of carnage behind me, because all the things I'm not addressing, not facing, not accepting, I'm taking out on other people.

Throughout history, spiritual people have challenged the premise that we are inherently bad; the question keeps arising, is there an alternative to that idea? To me, it's wonderful to realize that an alternative wouldn't occur to us unless we had some experience of it. So, I already have the experience that I'm seeking; now I just have to prove to myself that it is so. And that's what spiritual practice is.

In the process, I can expect that all my conditioning will rise up and attempt to convince me that what I am beginning to experience—my own goodness, the goodness of everything—is not true. The voices of egocentricity will rush right in to explain that it is really something else and what that means and why any intelligent person wouldn't fall for this kind of stuff. Most of us have to spend quite some time simply knowing the truth for ourselves before it no longer matters what our conditioning is saying.

But once I've seen the possibility that we are not inherently bad, that there is something other than what we've been taught, then I start looking for evidence of it. I sense it in nature, I hear it in something somebody says, I see it all around me, like little sparkles of goodness that bubble out from different places—I recognize that even though the circumstances vary, the sparkle is the same. The way I know it's what I'm looking for is that I feel it inside me when I find it outside me.

As with anything, once we accept that it is real, we see it everywhere and can't imagine how we missed it before. At a certain point, conditioning is perceived as a ludicrous and pathetic attempt to obscure the obvious—that the true nature of everything is compassion. Then we simply go forward in that knowledge, until there's nothing left outside that.

It all starts from the first recognition of that sparkle of goodness inside ourselves. We must pursue that with every cell of our being, every ounce of strength, every particle of hope and desire—all the time knowing that the pursuit of it is what keeps it elusive. The only thing I can compare it to is being in love, but it's the loving that is the point, not possession, because to possess it is to destroy the very aspect that is adored. It is the adoration itself that is the joy and excitement and bliss. So to pursue is everything; only a fool would want to possess it. And most of us go through a pretty long foolish period.

If we look at healthy children, what we often notice first is their energy. They're plugged in to life, they're going full speed ahead. Rhea, our new dog at the monastery, is the same—she's enthusiasm in a fur suit. She's not doing anything but being alive: she's not worrying, she's not blaming, she's not trying to control, she's not trying to be right, she's not trying to figure things out, she's not doing any of the stuff that saps the life force from us. Most of us give most of our life force to egocentricity, to feed conditioning. When we stop doing that, there's just pure vitality. I look at Rhea, and I see happiness. Of course, I can't actually know that she's happy, but I know she's really alive. If she steps on a thorn, she is as enthusiastic about that experience as she is about getting to go for a walk—she's jumping around and making noise and trying to pull it out—and she has that same wholehearted approach to everything. If you go away and leave her too long, she's fully present with that experience, too, whining and whimpering and groaning and looking forlorn. Then the instant you come back, all is forgiven, and all that energy is directed toward what happens next. And that's exactly how we can be.

In the Daily Recollection we repeat, "In this way I do most deeply vow to train myself," not, "In this way I do most deeply vow to train others." It's much more manageable when it's just ourselves. In Buddhism, instead of trying to save everybody else, each person is given one person to save: the one whose difficulties we know most intimately and can work with most directly.

At the same time, we also say, "The merit for all good acts I freely offer to all beings." What does "merit" mean here? I would guess goodness. The freedom, the joy, the bliss, whatever goodness comes from an action—may all beings share in that.

Cheri Huber

This book is based on discussions that took place at Southern Dharma Retreat Center near Hot Springs, North Carolina, during a Zen retreat devoted to the Buddhist precepts. The retreat was led by Cheri Huber; she was assisted by a monk (Greg) from the Zen monastery where she teaches.

The participants were mostly long-term Zen students who intended to accept the Buddhist vows in a formal ceremony at the end of the retreat, along with a few people who had already taken the vows and wished to renew them. These retreats are open also to students who want to learn about the precepts as well as people who are new to Zen practice.

The meditation hall at Southern Dharma, where the discussions took place, is an airy space defined by white walls, wood floor and ceiling beams, windows looking out into treetops, and skylights opening to sun and clouds. The room is furnished with dark brown meditation cushions and mats. Most of the time, meditators experience the room in silence: the living silence of birdsong virtuosos, insect symphonies, rain, wind, breath—the world of subtle sound that gets lost in talk. The words related here, it is important to remember, arose from and return to that silence.

1

There is

Not to lead a harmful life nor encourage others to do so

no separate self

Key:	Gratitude
Prohibition:	Not killing
Aspiration:	To live in harmony with all life and the environment that sustains it
Inspiration:	*There is no separate self*

CHERI: Most of you are here because you've been practicing this path for some time, and you are interested in accepting the precepts as a way to deepen your practice. Some of you are interested in finding out what the precepts are all about, and others of you probably signed up for a Zen retreat and have no idea what to expect. I would encourage every one of us to aim for that state of mind throughout this retreat and throughout life: not knowing what to expect, being open to something we cannot even imagine—because that is where this path leads us. I hope no one leaves here feeling that now they have some answers. Instead, what I would wish for us all is that we leave here able to question ever more deeply.

This will be like a regular Zen retreat in that our schedule

will have periods of sitting and walking meditation, with one
period of working meditation each day. When we sit on the
cushion, we are practicing being present. In walking meditation, we practice bringing that experience along as we move
around. In working meditation, we take it a step further,
bringing that same attentiveness to an activity. It is the
attentiveness that is important here—not finishing a task
and doing it perfectly or striving to achieve anything at all
except being completely present to what we're doing. So, in
the working meditation you approach it just as you do meditation on the cushion: every time your mind wanders, you
gently bring it back to the present, and you pay attention to
whatever happens.

A precepts retreat is different from a regular retreat in
that in the morning and in the evening we have a group
discussion. There are ten precepts and we have ten days, so
we'll examine one a day. Of course, it won't work out quite
that neatly, but that's roughly the plan. In addition to the
Ten Grave Prohibitive Precepts, there are the Three Pure
Precepts, which will also come into the discussions. On the
schedule you will notice some free time each day. I would
encourage you to use those periods to reflect on each of the
precepts as we consider them.

At some point, those of you who have participated for
the whole ten days will be asked if you wish to accept the
precepts formally at the end of the retreat. The decision as to
whether this is the appropriate time in your practice to take
these vows will be made in individual interviews with the
teacher.

Except for the discussions, we will observe silence. That
includes not reading or writing, unless it's part of an activity
we participate in together. For example, each morning we
recite the Daily Recollection, which consists of the basic
teachings of the Buddha, including the precepts. There are

copies available, and you might want to take one to keep.

So, let's jump right in. The first precept is "Not to live a harmful life, nor encourage others to do so."

RIC: My reaction is to want to know how you, as the teacher, interpret harmlessness. I wonder, "Is she going to expect me to give up eating meat?" Even though you say there is no right or wrong in the precepts, I suspect that they imply some judgment on my behavior—and that I'm wrong.

GREG: And in making that assumption, you just broke that precept.

RIC: You mean—that was a harmful judgment I just passed on myself?

GREG: Yes.

CHERI: So that precept is helpful to you already.

RIC: Ah—okay. [pause] Well, if that's how it works, then, about eating meat . . .

CHERI: The good news is that you can do anything you want to do. As that great Buddhist writer Christmas Humphreys said, we are punished *by* what we do, not because of what we do.

DENNIS: By the consequences of the act?

CHERI: I don't think that's it. My favorite story along these lines is about William Penn converting to Quakerism as an adult. He wore a sword, which was the custom of the day for gentlemen, and he recognized the contradiction in committing himself to a nonviolent spiritual path and wearing an instrument of destruction. So he went to the fellow who helped him convert and asked about it, and the fellow's response is the most Buddhist thing I've ever heard: "Wear it for just as long as you can."

For me, that's essential: do whatever you do, but pay attention to it. When we do something and pretend we're not doing it, we can cause harm without ever knowing how it happens. But with full awareness of our action, we quickly see its effects.

Do whatever you do—just pay attention to it.

RIC: A little voice in me says, "But doesn't she *really* think that one way is right and another is wrong?"

CHERI: *You* think there really is a right way and wrong way.

RIC: But isn't it possible that I could be paying full attention and come to a different conclusion from you?

CHERI: It wouldn't do you any good if I were to say yes or no to that. The only thing that would be helpful is for you to find out for yourself. That's the beauty of this practice for me: we find out for ourselves. So when I say you believe there's a right way and a wrong way, I'm suggesting that as a useful area for you to investigate.

You will often hear me or Greg or anyone involved in this practice say, "In my experience . . . ," or words to that effect. That's exactly what we have to offer—our own experience. And my experience is a work in progress, not a finished product.

JESSICA: In considering what is harmful, doesn't intent come into it? We can mean well and try hard, and sometimes we seem to do good, and other times we don't. For example, I was reading a book in the library, and a small something-or-other flew onto the page. I tried to blow it off, but it wouldn't blow. So I tried very gently to nudge it, and in the process I killed it. But my intent was to enable it to go on living.

CHERI: Those little creatures often don't nudge well, do they? Now, in a case like that, what beliefs might keep me from just propping the book open and leaving it there? A belief about the importance of my life compared to the life of the insect? Or that somebody seeing the book left like that might think I was careless or inconsiderate? There could be an interesting twist in this situation, if you think about it.

It may be hard to understand that you try to save the insect not for its sake but for yourself. Once you realize that, you no longer hold the expectation that it live happily ever after.

I learned that lesson in a terrible way. I had extricated a fly from something sticky it was caught in. You have to be careful because they are so fragile, and it took me forever to get this guy free. Then I set it down, got all its little legs on the floor, and was feeling good about this rescue effort, when up through the crack came a spider, and *thoomp*—that was the end of the fly. The point is that I'd better be doing what I'm doing for the well-being of my own heart, because I cannot know that it's going to be helpful to anybody else. As for rescuing insects, I just know that it makes me feel good. If I have a choice between reading a newspaper and saving a bug, I'm going to save the bug, because it gives me a happier outlook on life.

So, no guarantees. If I'm kind and polite to somebody in one interaction, I increase the odds that they're going to be kind and polite to me in the next interaction. But I cannot count on it, so it's much better if I am kind and polite just because I want to be. Otherwise, if they don't return the favor, I may conclude that there's something wrong with being kind and polite.

Harmlessness: what is it?

KAREN: The second part of this precept is harder for me, "not encouraging others"—the question of whether silence encourages or not, whether involvement helps or not. I would love to have something that tells me, "Do this, don't do that."

CHERI: In my experience, it is almost always a matter of not doing. We spend a great deal of time trying to figure out what we should do. But if we focus on stopping ourselves from doing the harmful thing, then the "not encouraging" almost always falls into place.

ELLEN: So it has nothing to do with trying to influence someone else?

CHERI: In my experience, it does not.

CYNTHIE: What about a situation that is dangerous, like someone close to you who is drinking and driving?

CHERI: For me, that raises the question of whose experience you're trying to take care of.

RIC: Can't we know that someone shouldn't drink and drive?

CHERI: What we think of as "knowing" is holding on to something we think applies universally so we don't have to be open to new situations.

The greatest caring we can offer others is trusting that they are equal to their life experience, whatever it may be.

MIRIAM: If someone involved in something harmful, like addiction, comes to you for assistance, where is the line between trying to control the person's behavior and encouraging the harmful activity?

CHERI: If we knew where that line was, we could show everybody, then they would get on the right side of the line, and we'd all be happy ever after. But since that won't work, I suggest that we explore the possibility that the greatest caring we can offer others is acknowledging their inherent adequacy—trusting that they are equal to their life experience, whatever it may be.

ELLEN: This afternoon during working meditation, the bugs were driving me nuts . . .

CHERI: The ones we call orifice gnats, that kamikaze into your eyes and mouth and up your nose?

ELLEN: And your ears. You can hear them in there, trapped. For a while I worked really fast and paced around to try to leave them behind. Then I tried slowing down, to make it easier for them to get in and get out again. But nothing worked. Finally this precept came to mind, and I thought about how many bugs had met their demise in my orifices, and how I was clearly not benefitting from this experience, and how the marginal benefit to the retreat center from the three yards of ditch I had managed to clean out really was not worth it. I thought about coming down and putting bug repellent on and going back, but then there wouldn't be any time left to work. Finally, I just came back, put my rake away, went to my tent and sat there and had all sorts of wonderful thoughts about other precepts. But all the while I was feeling selfish for not doing my work assignment and worried about whether that was okay or not. I'm still not sure, but I think it was more beneficial to both me and the bugs to not try to clean the ditch.

CHERI: Wasn't life simple before we started this precepts business—back when you could just swat bugs and be done with it?

KAREN: My parents just visited me, and it was one of the easiest times I've ever had with them, even though differences did arise. For example, transporting ants outside the house instead of killing them is not my father's idea of a reasonable thing to do, and he kept asking what I would do if we had fire ants like they do in Texas. I said I didn't know.

They kept trying to pin me into some reaction, but as long as I stayed with saying that I didn't know and not saying things back to them, it was actually pretty peaceful.

I did feel an impulse to try to get them to consider harmfulness in their lives. But that sounds as if I've found "The Way," which elevates me and separates us further. The only balance I could find was silence.

CHERI: Pointing out how other people are wrong does tend to close them to your perspective. In that situation—when if it's not fire ants, it's something else we have to fight against—I can't imagine anything better you could offer than to stay centered yourself, in the present moment, where there is no fear.

RIC: I'm less sure now than I was this morning about what harmlessness means, about what is harmful and what is not harmful.

CHERI: That sounds to me like great progress. If you came here tonight with a clearer sense of what is harmful and what is not, most likely you would have solidified whatever belief system you already had. I'm hoping we'll break down belief systems. I would love it if you went out of here saying, "Harmless, harmless, harmless: what *is* it?" With that attitude of mind, you'll be scrutinizing everything. You won't assume that you know what is so.

2 Not to take what is not given

Key:	Generosity
Prohibition:	Not stealing
Aspiration:	To freely give, ask for, and accept what is needed
Inspiration:	*There is no scarcity of resources*

MARY ELLEN: For me, "what is given" isn't clear. How do I know what is given to me?

CHERI: We want to establish rules so that we know, "This is mine, I have a right to this; I'm not sure about that; I'd have to ask about that; I don't ever get to have that." Then we would never have to be present to a situation. Even if we don't like it, we're willing to go along with a rule, railing against it or being depressed or defeated by it when necessary—anything rather than being present to our moment-by-moment experience.

Does it seem that it would be hard to be present all the time? What if you had to find out everything every moment?

Wouldn't that be a disaster for relationships? Each time you interacted with someone you would have to treat them as if you had just met them; you would have to be totally with them every time you were in their company.

But what is the alternative? Taking people for granted, pigeonholing them, dismissing them. And consider this: if I'm going to be really present every single moment of my life, to each person who is in my life, how much stuff can I be attending to in my mind at the same time? How many conversations can I keep up? How many grudges can I hold? How many fears about the future can I maintain? You can't keep it all going, can you? Not if you're going to be totally present to whatever is in front of you.

It seems to me that part of our belief system demands that we *not* be present to one another, *not* be in the moment, because if we are, all this mental structure we work so hard to maintain, this sense of ourselves as separate from all that is, which is egocentricity—that is going to collapse. And then where will we be?

The answer to that question is, free.

RIC: If "free" means not knowing what to say, not knowing how to act, losing all the things I carry with me into the next moment so I'll know how to behave—that terrifies me. If everything is gone—well, I guess I would like to know more about what "free" means.

CHERI: Do you want to know tonight, or shall we save that for tomorrow?

RIC: I'm guessing it will take more time than . . .

CHERI: Well, you just spend one more night in bondage, and then tomorrow we'll do freedom. But before you tuck yourselves in, here's a little bedtime story about taking what is given.

Old Zen monk happily living in a hut at the edge of town. Down the road come a man and a woman carrying a baby. When they get to the monk's hut, the woman thrusts the baby into the monk's arms and says to him, "You have disgraced our family. You got our daughter pregnant, and you have ruined our lives. This child is your responsibility!" The old monk says, "Is that so?" He takes the baby and cares for it. Years later, the same two people come down the road, this time with a very different attitude. They say, "Oh, we're so sorry, we were wrong. Our daughter lied to us. The father of the baby was a soldier, and he had gone to war, and she was afraid he would be killed. But now he's back, and they are getting married, and they want their child." And the old monk turns the child over to them and says, "Is that so?"

Now, if the monk had tried to keep a balance sheet on all of this, what would he have said on each occasion that would help him reconcile this great wrong that had been done to him by these people? But he didn't think of it in those terms. Here is the child, somebody needs to take care of it, they're giving it to him, fine. Now they want it back? It was never his in the first place. Fine.

That is freedom that cannot be disturbed.

What we want, and what we need

MARY: I've been thinking about trying to take power, and how I'm always putting myself on one side or the other of the power equation. I've had the experience of arguing with someone, and then the argument spontaneously collapsing under its own weight, and suddenly it was just funny. Then I realize that the whole system of power is a fantasy. All I have to do is step back, get centered, and there's nothing to argue about, there's no power to hold. It's only when I put myself in opposition to something—

CHERI: —that you try to maintain something. "When opposites arise, Buddha mind is lost." The moment you step into the world of duality, something must be maintained. There is an "I" and there is an "other." The moment you want something, you're already in trouble, because that is based on the illusion of separateness.

MARY: By wanting something, I'm assuming I don't have it.

CHERI: Yes, and then you're one down. You don't have, and someone else has.

MARY: But I really *don't* have a sports car.

CHERI: But that doesn't require you to want one.

ELLEN: The wanting may arise even when I don't want one. What egocentricity wants is just to want; it doesn't care about what it gets.

CHERI: Yes. Wanting is what maintains egocentricity, not getting. That's why we can want something, get it, and, without missing a beat, feel, "Yeah, but it's the wrong color. It's not big enough. There's a newer model. I was wrong; that really isn't what I want." Or, "I did want that then, but now what will really make me happy is this other thing." In Buddhism, this is called "seeking better accommodation."

Wanting and having have nothing to do with one another. They're completely separate processes.

ELLEN: But what I want often seems so basic, so necessary— not extravagant like a sports car.

CHERI: There is a great section in *The Screwtape Letters* where a woman wants a simple cup of tea, and she says, "Is that so much to ask?" But then we learn that it's a specific type of tea, brewed for exactly this amount of time, and served in a particular cup at a certain temperature by a certain person in a certain setting with a certain something on the side, and suddenly we've involved the whole universe. And she says, "Is that so much to ask?"

RIC: But what about a battered wife who says, "All I ask is not to be hit"—is that too much to ask?

CHERI: Are you asking if she's really asking that? If you are, my answer is that I doubt it.

RIC: Well, it's a request I would listen to and find reasonable.

CHERI: And yet, Ric, you've certainly worked with enough people to know that you could say, "Okay, then here's what to do," and what is the response? "Yes, but—."

RIC: So, something else may be going on?

CHERI: Right. I think it's a game we all play. I remember saying to myself in a moment of deep introspection, "All I want is to be loved." And then a little voice said, "More." It was a terrible moment of honesty, because what I was in fact saying was, "All I want is for you to love me more than you love you. All I really want is for you to choose me instead of you."

Is that too much to ask? Maybe it is. Is it too much to ask that I not be hit—while I continue to live with a violent person?

RIC: I see what you're saying. I'll have to think about it.

But for myself, I worry that no one will give to me. And if I can't take, I will have to ask for what I need, and maybe I won't get it. My fear is that I'll end up with nothing.

CHERI: Yes, we want to be in full control of everything we receive and don't receive. We assume there's not enough, that we need to actively try for our share or we won't get it.

Focusing on what we think we need keeps us from being present to what's already right here.

But in my experience, it's focusing on what we think we need that keeps us from being present to what's already right here. If I have something in my hand and I'm holding on to it, I can't receive anything else because my hand is already full. When I let that go, my hand is open to receive, and then I'm in a position to accept everything that's available.

The next step is the experience of true joy when it all just passes through your hand. So, holding on to anything limits us—and that includes the idea of not holding on to anything.

In this way I do most deeply vow to train myself.

3 Not to commit or participate in unchaste conduct

Key: Love

Prohibition: Not lusting

Aspiration: To give and accept affection
and friendship without clinging

Inspiration: *There is no scarcity of love*

CHERI: The more traditional wording of this precept is "not to participate in unlawful sexual intercourse." But, unlawful according to what law? In which state? That approach is probably not helpful in what we hope to accomplish by working with the precepts. The point is not what we can get away with.

MARY: I tend to think of "unchaste" only in terms of sexual conduct, but I looked it up in the dictionary, and it mentioned purity, which I find more meaningful. If I have sexual relations in the context of a legal marriage, and it's all focused on myself and there's no exchange there, there's no love, then to me that is unchaste. From society's point of view, it may be okay, but if there's no sincerity or compassion, then it isn't pure.

PATTI: If I can see what my motivation is in choosing an action, I have a better idea of whether it's pure in intent or not. Is it coming from fear or loneliness, or from a centered place?

ELLEN: My approach to this one is, if something doesn't feel as if it's leading away from suffering, then it's probably better not to participate in it.

KAREN: This precept prompts me to ask whether I am being responsible to myself, honoring myself in what I'm doing.

CHERI: So, what comes from a centered place feels pure; what doesn't come from a centered place feels impure, even if technically you're within the range of acceptable behavior. And so this precept can be helpful in drawing us back to a centered place.

RIC: Let's take the other side. If I feel that sex without commitment can be okay, when there's mutual consent and no exploitation but I don't know the other person, is that chaste or unchaste? Does it come back to how I define that, to what feels pure to me?

CHERI: The first thing would be to look at that very issue: what does purity mean to you? This opens up a whole realm of experience to be explored. What beliefs about sexuality do you hold on to? How do you decide about it? Do you pay attention to it? Are you really present with yourself, or do you leave yourself? These are good questions for anyone.

RIC: I'm thinking about how to pay attention without making judgments. I automatically picture someone saying that this is right, this is wrong, here's the rule. I know that fighting with that kind of judgment means it's very important to me, but I'm still hung up on it.

CHERI: Yes, the judgment lives within you. Once we realize that we're projecting that judgment onto others, but that the judgment is really within ourselves, then we can work with it.

This is not to say that much of society wouldn't also make judgments about anonymous sex, because lots of people can get fired up on that subject. But that's not the point. The point is how I feel about it. If I feel clarity within myself about an issue, I don't care what other people think about it, I don't tune in to their judgment. So any time I think someone is judging me, I can trace that back to myself and know that I've got concerns with that issue.

RIC: I've noticed that my own judging can actually maintain a certain behavior. When I let go of the judging and ask myself what it would mean to be clear and centered in regard to this behavior, how I could be fully present to it, then the issue tends to fall away.

CHERI: That's one of those things that seems totally backwards when we first hear it. I often tell people that when they stop hating themselves, they won't need to abuse drugs or alcohol or tobacco or sex. We do those behaviors so we can continue to hate ourselves—not the other way around.

Where to look for love and respect

JAN: There are two words I associate with this precept: on the one hand "desire," and on the other "respect." In my mind I see a line with a person on either side, me and somebody else. My desire can cause me to step over that line and to take what's not given, to go after something. To me, crossing that line is committing unchaste conduct; participating in unchaste conduct is when I allow somebody else to come over that line in their desire for me.

The respectful action would be to wait at the line. That's important to me, meeting somebody at the line, whether it's sex or anything else—not grabbing and not allowing myself to be grabbed, to be objectified. I often suffer in sex or in other interactions when I'm being treated as an object and I'm allowing it; all of a sudden I find myself aware that I don't feel very human, although I knew all along what was happening.

CHERI: Underneath that, for me, at a deeper level, is the sadness because we have abandoned ourselves in the belief that somebody else has something we're lacking. If we stay stuck in fighting against the behavior, we'll never get to what's underneath it. But if we call it off on either side of the battle—dropping the behavior, *or* dropping the resistance to it—we can see what's operating underneath. It might be the fear of *not* being someone's object: what if they go find another object? Or the fear of not being able to possess something that causes you to have a certain experience of yourself. We get into these arrangements with other people and fail to see how we both suffer as a result.

Many of us believe it's not possible to be present to the moment and have a relationship with somebody. We assume that if you and I don't need one another, there would be no reason to be together. If it's not motivated by need and deprivation and fear, why would I have anyone else in my life? Well, how about because I enjoy them?

JAN: I'm having to learn what it means to be in a relationship out of something other than need. I can say I love somebody and we enjoy each other, but deep down I know that's not why I got into it.

CHERI: It's clinging and grasping all the way, believing we're not all right without it. With children, as you know with your own little boy, the process of socialization encourages him to turn away from his heart, his own sense of who he is, and getting him to turn toward you and his father for his well-being. And that's part of doing the very best we can for a child. He has to fit into society; he has to learn that this is the way we eat and this is where we do that activity and so on. Before long he won't look to himself at all to know how he should be. He'll be focused outward, first on his parents, and then on teachers and other adults, and eventually everything he needs to know will come from out there.

There's a deep grieving when we abandon ourselves for the approval of others so we can receive from others what we think we need. We will happily participate in that which is unchaste in order to get those needs met. It doesn't occur to us to look within ourselves. But now here we are in spiritual practice trying to go back and reclaim ourselves, and it is scary. It seems as if we're going to have to give up everything out there, and that we can't do that and survive.

There's a deep grieving when we abandon ourselves for the approval of others to get what we think we need. Now here we are in spiritual practice trying to go back and reclaim ourselves.

I think the best thing we can offer to anyone, especially children, is the fact that we are doing this work ourselves. We're trying to pay attention, we're trying to let go of beliefs and assumptions about life and about ourselves and one another. The fact that you're in a grown-up body doesn't mean you know anything. I don't think it makes children insecure to be told what they already know very clearly—that we know nothing. I think it builds their confidence in adults when we at least have the ability to acknowledge what is so.

GREG: There's a way in which all the precepts can be stated as "not to pretend to be a separate self." And it's especially so with this precept.

The Power of Commitment

CHERI: Until we make a commitment, we tend to keep looking for something better. In Buddhism we call this "seeking better accommodation." It applies to our whole lives, but it is especially pertinent to this precept.

Our conditioning is such that we don't focus on what we have, we focus on what we want. And we don't think of what we want as including what we already have; what we want is by definition something we lack. Egocentricity is focused on loss, lack, deprivation, dissatisfaction, fear, problems, the past, the future—all of which keeps us out of the moment, which is the only place where we could have everything we want. Only by committing to something can we open up to receiving it. If we commit to a relationship, then what is available to us is the exploration of what is there, rather than the endless pursuit of what is not there. That's the power and benefit of making a commitment.

In a relationship, people tend to think of commitment as meaning sexual. But I think it's much broader. It speaks to purity, to morality. To me "pure" is associated with whatever is fully present in the moment, and "impure" is associated with responding from our conditioning, which is the realm of egocentricity and suffering. It has nothing to do with the nature of a relationship: whether it is within a marriage, or between a man and a woman of the same race and comparable ages, or any of the strictures we want to apply in an effort to enforce our own belief systems about what is right. In spiritual practice based on developing awareness, belief systems presented as moral issues are irrelevant.

The commitment I am talking about is to awareness— not to another person or a certain time frame or type of situation, but to spiritual practice. People will tell me that they are in a bad relationship, but they don't want to leave because it will hurt the other person and because they have the idea that leaving will be breaking a precept. I want them to see that they may be harming themselves, and the fact that they aren't considering themselves is a part of social conditioning, not part of awareness practice.

Now, I do not advise anyone to leave a relationship or to stay in a relationship. In terms of spiritual practice, it doesn't matter which we do. All that matters is that we pay attention and find out what our conditioning is and how that causes us to suffer. If we leave this relationship, we will most likely get right into another one, and we'll continue to operate from the same conditioning, causing the same suffering.

I was suggesting this to a woman who had left many relationships and was thinking of leaving her present one, and she looked increasingly horrified as I talked. I think what horrified her is the prospect of doing with conscious awareness what she has been doing unconsciously. Personally, I would rather do whatever I'm doing with my eyes wide open and see what it is and where it leads, see the suffering involved for myself and everyone else, since being unconscious simply allows my conditioning to play itself out who knows how many more times.

If we accept as our working premise that the present moment contains all that is, was, or ever could be, that everything that is possible is available in this moment, then the only way I can manage to miss that is by not being in this moment. Let's say I'm in a relationship and we're getting along fine in every way except that we don't communicate well. We have a lot of common interests, we like the same things in a house, we both want children, but when it comes to talking about things that are deep and intimate and important to us, we just can't communicate. When I try talking to you, I am thinking, "Same old struggle . . . If only he . . . This is hopeless." So my efforts to communicate drive us further apart, entrenching me deeper in my beliefs and assumptions and projections, my little view of the world, reinforcing my sense of being right. To me, that is "impure"— to have the whole focus of the relationship be whatever is wrong between us.

Purity lies in making the commitment to bring conscious awareness to this situation, to experiencing the oneness that we are. Let's say that finally I realize that this relationship *is* my spiritual practice. It takes two people not to be able to communicate, so clearly I am one half of this situation. I stay, because I want to see what is available for me here. Now, instead of finding something wrong between us, I am truly, purely, wholeheartedly committed to being present with you. I want to see as clearly as I can everything that keeps me separate from you: the beliefs I maintain, the conditioning I bring, the projections I have, all the suffering I cause through holding on to these egocentric positions. Now I'm going to use my awareness practice to let those go so that I can be fully present in the relationship.

In this way I do most deeply vow to train myself.

4 Not to tell lies nor practice believing the fantasies of authority

There is

no need to hide

the truth

Key: Honesty

Prohibition: Not lying

Aspiration: To see and act
in accordance with what is

Inspiration: *There is no need to hide the truth*

MARY: I think of myself as an honest person, but if I pay attention I'm surprised to see how many lies I tell. Mostly, it's in response to what I think other people want or expect.

ELLEN: I often feel that if I open my mouth it will be clear to everyone that what I really want or who I really am is not what I want to project. And I can't risk the loss of that identity, so I don't say anything at all.

CHERI: So the unspoken lie serves to maintain the illusion. Even though—and here's the great tragedy of being human—saying exactly what's going on with you might enable you to receive what you truly want.

We might as well relax and be who we are. We put so much energy into hiding, because we believe we have to be a certain way in order to survive. But we're really no good at it; we're the only ones fooled. People who love us know all our failings anyway and it doesn't bother them, and people who don't like us base their dislike on the very qualities we're so diligently trying to keep hidden.

RODNEY: Often people who love you participate in the dynamics of hiding those things. And when you are unaware of your effort to deceive, they will collude to keep it out of your awareness.

CHERI: This is not to imply that we should call up everyone we know and tell them the truth about themselves.

ELIZABETH: So what are we saying—that sometimes it's okay not to tell the truth?

CHERI: I would never say that it's okay not to tell the truth, but I hope that everybody would look carefully at what it *means* to tell the truth, and what it *means* to lie.

For me, to tell the truth about myself to myself seems critical, and then to tell the truth about myself in whatever occasions I want to tell the truth. The part that's shakiest for me is that we are conditioned not to tell the truth about ourselves, but to tell the so-called truth about others, which I think leads to more harm than good. That's when paying attention to motivation is helpful, looking at it in light of the first precept.

BECKY: This morning I caught myself in this ridiculous lie to myself. During meditation before breakfast I was hungry, and this thought went through my mind: "I hate seven-grain cereal." But that isn't true at all. I have no idea where that voice came from.

CHERI: So much for that authority, right?

MELINDA: In classic cases of abuse, the authority figure is never questioned because of the belief that that person is there to protect us. The same is true within ourselves, where the authority is egocentricity. Believing that it offers protection, we have an investment in not questioning its intentions.

CHERI: Yes, because if I were somehow able to rid myself of this authority, then I'd be alone. The relationship may be painful, but it's familiar.

MELINDA: And in an abusive situation, the only way to be good is to acknowledge how bad you are. If you don't acknowledge that, you're really bad. That also applies with ego.

CHERI: Furthermore, you must never defend yourself. So there are precious few ways out of this situation. This practice is one of the few ways out, and it works because we don't try to change anything about the dynamic, we simply watch it happen.

Let's take a simple example of the kind of lie most of us tell fairly frequently: someone calls me on the phone and I don't want to talk to them. I may tell myself I should just go on and talk, but I feel guilty because I'm lying. Usually we stay stuck in that kind of duality—doing the "right" thing but feeling guilty—rather than going into it more deeply to see what's actually there. In fact, that's the time to get out the magnifying glass and see if we can discover the authority that is operating in us.

The phone has rung, the person is on the line. What if I ask them to hold on a moment? Then I can stop and notice what's going on—which is, I don't want to do this, I don't want to say I don't want to do it, and I'm afraid to say what I do want. What exactly am I afraid of? Maybe it's that that person won't like me. If I keep asking questions, keep look-ing, I can end up with something as dire as being friendless and homeless and helpless—the survival fears of a very young child. Those kinds of fears, and the behaviors intended to protect us, come from voices of authority—our childhood conditioning—that once served a purpose in our lives but now serve only to keep us fearful.

So, we've uncovered this whole complex of conditioning. The Buddha talked about it as knots tied in a silk scarf. Rather than trying to untangle the knots, we tend to go right on telling ourselves, "I should be different, but I'm not; I feel hopeless"—trapped in an abusive situation with the ego as the authority figure.

What if we stayed present to the moment and said, "This is not a good time for me to talk?" That would be answering to a different authority—the moment. Sometimes I may say something like this, "Gosh, I just don't feel like talking now, and I don't even know why." If the other person is willing to stay with me through that process, I can explore it then and there, see in the moment exactly what it is, talking through it in the actual situation. An experience like that can change the whole direction of our interaction; a conversation that would have led to separation actually brings us closer. Instead of allowing some amorphous feeling that I haven't identified to come between me and somebody else, so that I end up feeling bad about both of us, I allow myself to be vulnerable in the moment and end up more connected to myself and to them.

In the moment, there is nothing that is not the truth.

With telling lies or any conditioned behavior, it's important to sit still with it just as it is so I can recognize it. Once I've made a mess, the tendency is to jump in and clean it up so I don't have to face the reality of it. And the next thing I know, I'm in the same mess again. Now, the question I want to answer is, how did I get here? So, first I sit still with the magnitude of the mess, then I watch myself clean it up, then

I watch myself begin to make the mess again. I keep watching that, without going to sleep at any point in the process.

From the point of view of our conditioning, there is lying and not lying, and we become obsessed with whether something is true or false. We want to form a rigid system, so we will know what is right and what is wrong. But if I say I work very hard at not lying, that itself is a lie. A very small part of me is even conscious of it, a very small part of the time. The rest of the time I am lost in lies, because I am operating out of conditioning that is nothing but belief systems: I say things I've never examined, don't know, don't understand. And within all that, part of me has this great concern for whether something is the truth or a lie. When we step back from it, it's absurd: conditioning itself is a lie, and it is only in the dualistic world of lies that we could hold a notion of lying and not lying. In the moment, however, there is nothing that is not the truth.

Truth as inner authority

LINDA: Is there a more standard way of phrasing "the fantasies of authority" part of this precept?

CHERI: This version of the precepts is somewhat more complex than versions you usually see. In my experience, the wording encourages people to consider that they may not know what the precept is about, rather than simply assuming that they do know. The second part of these two-part precepts is an aspect we're likely to overlook with a strict literal interpretation like, "Don't lie."

For me, the precepts are koans. The Zen koan is a spiritual puzzle that cannot be resolved with the intellect. Spirituality cannot be pursued intellectually. Oh, it can be—

it is by almost everybody. But we can't get there that way. Once we've understood all there is to understand intellectually, we find we're in the same place we were when we started.

RODNEY: I think we surrender to authority out of a sense of helplessness. Most of what I've learned about all of these matters has been from reading, and I am very attached to books by certain authors because they have taught me lessons that I would never have arrived at myself. So I honor and respect them and grant them authority.

CHERI: It's important to consider that those people simply said something that allowed you to realize something, and that the realization is completely your own. Otherwise you believe there's something outside you that somebody else brought to you. But it was simply a matter of holding up a mirror; those authors are projections of yourself. You can know this because if a particular thought or sentence or paragraph you read were a universal truth, then every one who read it would experience that. But that's not the case. You may have an experience of understanding through reading, or you may have the same understanding sitting on the cushion, or you may have it while you're sweeping the floor. If you had an awakening experience while sweeping the floor, you wouldn't feel a need to honor the authority of the broom.

Now, a person might be tempted to feel something like honoring the meditation hall, or even the cushion—to hold the idea that something happens because of certain circumstances. We like ritual, we like things in neat little packages that we can refer back to. But I would suggest that you examine a relationship like that and see what actually is going on.

JUNE: I've been having an interesting lesson with authority in the last few days. I've never been to a retreat before, and I came late so I didn't get any instructions. I tend to be intimidated by authority, but I said to myself, "Let's see if I can fit in without being intimidated."

Initially, I felt separate from everybody else. At the first sitting, I didn't have a copy of the Daily Recollection to read, and I tried to read this other sheet, but it wasn't the right one. Somehow, instead of being self-conscious and embarrassed, I thought, "I'm part of the group, we're all here for the same reasons. I don't have to read the words, I just can listen to them. I'll pretend everybody is saying these words to me."

Then during the meditation when I heard someone walking around, I had no idea what was happening. I could hear the footsteps coming toward me and then stop and then start coming closer. Then someone touched my back and helped me straighten my posture. I realized it must be Greg, and—well, everything was okay after all.

The most interesting thing was, my cushion was facing one of the screens, and when my mind would drift off, my body would begin to fall forward. Then my head would jerk, and that would bring my attention back. I was afraid that I would actually go to sleep and fall against the screen. But I thought that through and decided that if I knocked the screen over, nothing terrible would happen. No authority would punish me. And that would be something important to learn.

So my anxiety about authority just disappeared, and somehow everything was perfect. In fact, it's wonderful. I'm actually glad I came late.

CHERI: I'm glad we didn't interfere by trying to take care of you. It is also my experience of life that it's all perfect. I often have the kinds of thoughts I think you were describing—that all of this has been arranged for my benefit, it's all being done for my spiritual practice. The right person is always there at the right time. Someone says something, and I may not like it then, but it unfolds into exactly what I need to learn. It's like a huge stage with actors coming on and acting out these scenes just so I can understand how I cause myself to suffer and how to let go of it. Yet we spend so much time trying to figure out what's wrong instead of taking advantage of the gifts we are constantly given.

GREG: Here's a fantasy of authority. For over a year, I've been head of the construction crew at the monastery. Sometimes I believe I am truly in charge, and then I get upset when the others don't do what they are supposed to. The fact is that I don't know how to build this building, but it's not helpful to just muddle around, so I try to act like I know what I'm doing. But I'm the only one who gets caught up in believing I'm in charge.

CHERI: Maybe the building will get built, maybe it won't. When Greg, as the master builder, has trouble with the crew, I'm brought in as the authority. And then it gets really interesting, because I'm not confused at all about whether or not I'm in charge.

ACKER: You're—not in charge?

CHERI: No, I'm not. And the monks often don't like it that I take that view of life. There will be tremendous pressure on me to make a decision about something, and I will sit and look, but as long as there's no clarity about a direction, the answer is, we do nothing. With deadlines and building permits and inspections, people can get very nervous because now we're dealing with the law, we're talking about "real" authorities. But the response is still the same: I don't know. So there's nothing to do. I'm certainly not going to make a decision just because I feel pressured. What if they take our permit away from us? Then they will; what can I do about that?

Regardless of what happens, I would rather trust life and stay centered and live from that point of clarity. I suspect that when I feel I most need help, rules will be of no use to me. At the moment of death, how the county authorities feel about me is not going to sustain me. As for the fear that something could happen to me, if I am holding that fear, the worst has already happened.

RIC: I watch myself fight with authority a lot, and with this precept at first I thought, ah, this justifies my struggle. Then I looked a little harder and I saw that fighting authority is being every bit as attached to believing it as automatically following it. What I'm wondering now is how to listen to you or read Buddhism or discuss these precepts without setting them up as one more authority—to either fight against or automatically agree with?

CHERI: Supposedly when people came to study with the Buddha, he would say, "Believe nothing that I say." And I add to that, "Believe nothing that *you* say." Then perhaps we can start out in an open place where you're not looking to me as an authority, but you're also not looking to yourself as an authority. Without any authority at all, maybe we can simply explore what's here.

We're so accustomed to being students, to assuming that somebody—or, depending on the subject, almost everybody—knows more than we do. And so often we don't really look because we assume it would be easier just to go to an authority.

This particular spiritual path would be up a creek if the Buddha had approached it that way, because the fact of the matter is, nobody else knew. The Buddha kept saying, "There's something else here—what is it?" He asked everybody and he studied and read, but he didn't find the answer. Finally he said, "Well, then, I'll have to figure it out myself.

If nobody else knows, or nobody else has this question, or other people have this question but they seem to have settled for whatever answers they have, and these answers are unsatisfactory to me, I guess I'll just have to keep looking." It's a good model.

MIRIAM: What was he asking?

CHERI: The same kinds of things we're asking. What's the use of living when life is simply all of this suffering? If we must face old age, sickness, and death, and there's no way around it, what is the point? Surely there must be something more to life than living until you get sick and die. And that's kind of the question we're all asking, whether we formulate it in quite that way or not.

In this way I do most deeply vow to train myself.

5 Not to use intoxicating drinks or narcotics nor assist others to do so

There is no need to hide from the truth

Key: Awareness

Prohibition: Not clouding

Aspiration: To embrace all experience directly

Inspiration: *There is no need to hide from the truth*

CHERI: Well, have we beaten that last precept to death? What's the next one?

FAINT VOICE: Substance abuse.

CHERI: "Not to use intoxicating drinks or narcotics nor assist others to do so." So, there's no particular reason people weren't rushing into discussion on this one?

DENNIS: The Daily Recollection says "not to *misuse*."

CHERI: Oh, you got an old copy.

RIC: Let's go with that one.

CHERI: But that wouldn't get you anywhere, would it? Not to use, or not to misuse—we can explore it from both perspectives. As far as I'm concerned, they are exactly the same.

CYNTHIE: But does the precept say "use" or "misuse?"

CHERI: The way we usually say it is, "Not to use intoxicating drinks or narcotics." At one time we tried "not to misuse" because people were concerned about someone having a terminal illness not being able to take anything for the pain because it would break this precept.

GREG: For me, one aspect of this precept goes back to not harming. I explored drinking and using drugs long enough to see how it was harmful to my body, and I didn't want to do it any longer.

Another aspect of it is making a commitment to being here, being present. Drinking and using drugs is another way of looking elsewhere or wanting things to be different, which is based on the assumption that there's something wrong with what's happening.

If I'm keeping a precept because I'm afraid not to, I'm not keeping a precept, I'm just afraid.

JESSICA: Since "use" seems so categorically prohibitive, why isn't "misuse" a better word?

CHERI: Wouldn't we need to scrutinize just as carefully a decision to use something? If I'm keeping a precept because I'm afraid not to, I'm not keeping a precept, I'm just afraid.

CHRIS: Even if you have the word "use" in there, it doesn't necessarily stop an individual from interpreting it as "misuse." So the language is not the most important thing.

LINDA: I feel that the language can reflect very different ways of looking at it. Once in a while I like to drink a little beer or wine, and when I hear the precept as, "Do not use intoxicating substances," I think, "Ever?" I don't get intoxicated, so

I would prefer this to read, "Do not become intoxicated."

GREG: Or it could be that I don't want anybody to tell me I can't drink—because one of the fundamental addictions is being in charge, being in control.

RIC: Yes, my reaction to this precept is that I want the right to drink if I want to. But when I consider the reasons I want to drink, it is to numb pain or to leave an experience or lessen inhibitions so I can do something another part of me doesn't approve of.

Also, I realize there are a lot of other activities the word "intoxicating" can apply to. Sex, overworking, anything that gives me a rush so that I'm away from whatever is happening. I can even use helping somebody else to escape how I am hating myself about something. All of those things are intoxicating.

CHERI: Yes. And I'm surprised that no one has brought up caffeine and sugar.

JOHN: I mentioned them silently to myself.

CHERI: In another retreat, in the context of this precept, someone talked about tea, morphine, watching television, and reading—quite a spectrum there. That's a big hint that it's not the intoxicant itself but our own process of addiction, of using whatever the substance or experience is to maintain a certain identity that keeps us out of the present moment. Again, it's not what, but how. And a good thing to look at is the intention behind the act. Is it conscious or unconscious? Does it lead toward awareness or away from awareness, toward suffering or away from suffering?

MARY ELLEN: I feel so virtuous about not using caffeine that that in itself keeps me out of the present moment. I have all these rationalizations about why I don't and why it's good for me, but what it comes down to is that I like my image of myself when I don't do it. It's the flip side of doing it, and it keeps me out of the present moment just as much as doing it would.

MARY: In other words, it makes you feel holy not to do this thing.

CHERI: And since you know people who do indulge in it, we could say "holier than thou."

Unfortunately, I no longer drink diet cola—and I say "unfortunately" because it was one of the best teaching tools I had. I've thrown more people into a state of spiritual panic over diet cola. Now I just carry my Happy Donuts coffee mug, which elicits some of the same attitudes about what a spiritual teacher should be like. I bring that up because obviously if we have those attitudes and beliefs about someone else, we have them about ourselves. I mean, everybody knows that a spiritual teacher should live up to different standards than everybody else, higher standards—the standards we would set for ourselves except that we're not up to it. Right?

JESSICA: A problem I have with this precept is that it seems capricious, in that only alcohol and narcotics are mentioned. Both of those are depressants; are we to assume that hallucinogens and stimulants are okay? My sense of what this precept is about is that we don't want to cloud our minds in any way that will take us from the immediate perception of the moment. So to single out certain substances doesn't seem to make sense.

GREG: Another version you often hear from people who want to drink is, "Not to sell the wine of delusion."

GENE: Where do you buy that?

GREG: Just about everywhere!

KAREN: This precept has me look at anything I might get addicted to in my life, anything I think I have to have. If I find myself glued to a notion that something has to be a certain way, that's a warning that I should shift things around.

CHERI: Here we can see the "stupefying" aspect in a different way: the addiction itself is stupefying, the attachment rather than the substance.

> *The addiction itself is stupefying— the attachment rather than the substance.*

Growing up, I was the kind of kid who was always reading. I read in the bathtub, I walked into walls reading. I used reading like a narcotic; since I didn't like how my life was, I would indulge in reading to transport myself into another reality. In the monastery, not reading was one of the hardest things for me, and that was when I saw what an addiction it was. And when I caught myself finding excuses to go to the grocery store so I could read product information panels, I realized that it wasn't so much what I read as the process of reading. Until reading was withdrawn from my life, there had been no awareness of what was going on—it was like drinking alcohol because the mind is addicted to the escape aspect of it but having no awareness of its effect on the body. So that experience was very helpful to me; it's always good to know for ourselves how any behavior affects the whole system rather than operating from a belief that we should or should not do something.

GENE: In applying this precept, would you make a distinction between, say, a shaman of a South American Indian tribe using a drug to contact animal spirits before going on a hunt and people who smoke a couple of joints and get a pizza and watch "Raiders of the Lost Ark?"

CHERI: I can relate a lot more to the second one, if that's what you mean. But I truly don't care what either group is doing. The only thing I examine in regard to the precepts is my own life.

GENE: I guess for me it's a matter of intent. One person is using this substance as a vehicle for spiritual growth, the other for intoxication.

CHERI: Or, as far as we can know, for spiritual growth.

Conditioning tells us that everything is either/or. We've got to decide what is the right thing to do, which means we have to sacrifice this other thing that we really want to do. Since we can't pull that off, what happens is that we do one thing while believing we shouldn't do it; wanting to be one way and being another; trying to do this and hating ourselves for not doing it; on and on. If we watch that process long enough, it loses its grip on us.

What we're moving toward is living in compassionate awareness all the time. As we bring compassionate awareness to everything we're doing, we see through these convoluted illusions that we've been living by, and we will no longer want to do that—but not because it makes us good or it's the right thing. I'm convinced that if you gave a three-year-old a choice between taking drugs to have an altered experience or just being present to life, he or she would choose to be present to life. It feels better, it's more natural, it's more real, it's more fun. We do all these other things because we are no longer able to be present to ourselves in a joyful way. When we are able to be fully present to life, we don't want to do things that take us away from that.

That's the beginning of freedom. And what we need to keep in mind about freedom is that it is free. It's expansive. It's not a connect-the-dots kind of experience in which you follow certain steps to get the one right answer. Anything is possible, everything is available in that spaciousness. There's constant change. It can be disorienting to the part of us that wants to remain small and contracted and understood and controlled and safe. My image of it is being on rollerblades in a room full of ball bearings. You want to be flexible and alert, ready to move in any direction at any time, and then to change direction in a flash. If that process is appealing to you, if you can see that it's exciting, if you can feel how alive it is, if you are willing to learn to let go and relax into the movement, then your interest in being right, safe, and under control begins to fall away.

ACKER: I use various kinds of intoxication, from coffee to sugar to alcohol to overwork, to escape the moment. When I get up in the morning, the only way to make myself go to work is to drink coffee. In the middle of the day when things get rough, there's Ben and Jerry's ice cream to keep me going—

CHERI: A discriminating addict, and politically correct! But it's not helpful to lose our compassion for ourselves with this issue. Again, we're talking about whether I am able to be present to myself in this moment: am I here, or am I out there? That's the movement we're always exploring with the precepts, not determining once and for all whether I am a good person or a bad person.

CYNTHIE: To me, it's not restricting your use of an intoxicant but seeing how it perpetuates your suffering. It actually isn't a treat if you look at it carefully enough.

CHERI: That's a good thing to pay attention to. Every room I sit in is filled with people who have accomplished everything they want to accomplish, done all the things they were supposed to do to be happy, and they're not, so now what? This is the point at which many people become willing to explore spiritual possibilities.

People complain to me about their jobs, as if somebody

forces them go to work. They got way more education than any human being needs, then out of all of the jobs possible, they selected this one and felt absolutely ecstatic to get it. But before long they take the attitude that they're being mistreated because they have to go to work, and yet they stay in the job. I like to ask people to consider questions like, how long would you do that job if suddenly you were going to be paid minimum wage? Or, how long would you do your job if you never had any time off? If you didn't get to go out to eat? If you didn't get to buy yourself presents? We begin to get a sense of how we're constantly playing these things off one against the other: we'll do this, because the payoff is this; we'll do this amount of work, but we have to be rewarded in this way.

As Cynthie observes, these things we become so dependent on are not really treats. Yet when we feel we are living lives that are not what we want, the coffee or the ice cream or the dinner out or the new gadget appears as a very bright spot in an otherwise dismal grind.

Often we give up an addictive form of treats without addressing the stresses that caused us to turn to that behavior. And that can be just one more act of cruelty: now we're going to take away what we perceive as a pleasure while we go ahead and live the life that is so unsatisfactory that it caused us to overindulge in that pleasure.

If we don't get to have coffee in the morning and Ben and Jerry's ice cream in the middle of the day and who knows what in the evening after starting off like that, then we want to work in a place where we don't feel that we have to fortify ourselves to go there and survive it. It's important to examine both sides of it, instead of seeing ourselves as bad for having those things. To say that we should go to that miserable job that is so stressful and get nothing except going there—that seems kind of harsh. I would wonder about the motivation behind that kind of decision, as opposed to considering what would be the truly compassionate approach for this person's life.

A concern that often arises with this precept is about painkillers. Now, consider this. You could lie down and go to sleep wherever you are when the time comes. But you don't, because it could be uncomfortable there on the porch, say, if that's where you happened to be when you get tired. Or when you need clothes, you could walk into a store and buy the first three things you encountered and wear them, but if you started in the children's department those clothes wouldn't fit and you wouldn't be able to function very well. We work it out to have a comfortable arrangement for sleeping, we choose comfortable clothes to wear, and in fact we constantly try to avoid pain and discomfort.

Now, what can we learn from noticing where we draw the lines about what's not acceptable in that respect? Who makes the decision that with a physical condition that causes me to be in pain I shouldn't take a painkiller? To me the precepts would be valuable if they did nothing else but ferret out that voice that says, "I shouldn't . . ." or, "A spiritual person always . . ." or, "I have to . . . ." When we talk about considering the precepts in our lives, we mean without the input of that voice.

Pay attention, see what happens, look for those voices of authority. You might start with something like drinking coffee: see how you feel before, see how you feel during, see how you feel afterwards. Switch to decaffeinated coffee, then notice what voices arise in you, what they tell you—just to see who the players are and what their concerns are. Don't drink coffee and see what happens, then drink it and see what happens. Drink it in the afternoon instead of the morning. If you use milk and sugar, change to black, then vice versa. Make it into an experiment. Your purpose is to get to know yourself.

Who is saving whom?

DENNIS: I wonder about the "assisting others" part of this precept. It seems like enough for me to work on staying clear myself, and to add the aspect of other people makes it really hard. I think of instances when saying something about somebody's alcohol abuse, or not saying something about it, have essentially the same effect—none. In fact, either approach can encourage it.

GREG: I see so often that the only way to stop a behavior is to accept it just as it is. So, if someone has trouble with intoxicants, is it possible for me to be completely open to that, to not try to change them? That's something I can always do. I can't know what effect it will have, but at least I won't have made the other person out to be inadequate and hopeless, which is what often happens when people try to help someone change.

MARY: I would want to be sure that I'm doing it for myself. An example in my life was living with an active alcoholic and deciding not to engage in arguments when the other person was intoxicated. I didn't make that decision so that this person would see the light and quit drinking. I did it because it was painful for me to continue that behavior, and I finally realized that I didn't have to.

CHERI: What you're pointing at is the need to act completely from your own heart. In that sense, your decision had nothing to do with the other person.

DENNIS: But I do want the other person to stop.

CHERI: That's the hook we bite time and time again. The

expectations, the hidden hopes in things we do. Even with spiritual practice, we might have a hope that it's going to affect somebody else. "Maybe they'll start meditating too, and then their life will get better."

What about the opportunity that person offers you to let go of your belief in someone else's inadequacy? What if the other person is the bodhisattva, whose role is to help *you* awaken?

RODNEY: I've heard about a Buddhist priest who actually drinks and takes drugs with addicts in trying to help them end their suffering. Apparently it's a therapeutic technique and part of his ministry.

CHERI: Let's say I am considered mentally ill. I've had a breakdown and I've attempted suicide. Rodney, as my therapist, is terrified of suicide—suicide in general and my suicide in particular, because I'm his client and it doesn't look good for his reputation if I kill myself. So here we are, having this interaction that Rodney hopes will be helpful.

Before I reached this state, I was more or less like Rodney—following all the rules and working at a regular job. Then I saw the light and realized that that was completely nuts. But I couldn't see any way out of it, so I tried to kill myself. Now, in front of me is Rodney, sitting there in his suit and tie. I know that life, and I don't want it.

The only thing that can influence me is Rodney coming to where I am. He could do that by simply asking me, "What's it like to try to kill yourself? Do you remember what you were thinking about? How did that feel?" The one thing that will get through to me is for him to connect with my experience. If he says, "I know that. I've been there, too, but I don't think I'd have guts enough to shoot myself," or, "What I tried was so-and-so," or, "I went through six bad marriages," or whatever, then I know he has some idea of what I'm experiencing.

Being unafraid to drink or take drugs with an addict— to be where that other person is— could make quite an impact.

He's been where I am, but he's gone back, so I can guess he knows something I don't know, since I haven't made the trip back yet. But now I'm thinking I might want to follow him.

That's why the best drug and alcohol counselors are ex-addicts. A person being unafraid to drink or take drugs with an addict— especially a person who has taken vows on the issue—that degree of willingness to be where the other person is could make quite an impact.

The only thing I think we have to offer someone else is our own centeredness, our own being all right, and knowing beyond a doubt that they're all right. If I know that about myself in a way that lets me know that about everyone, I speak with true authority, in the sense of knowing what is so. But if I don't have that experience of being all right, if I am afraid for you because I am afraid for me, all I have to offer you is my fear. "Maybe if you quit drinking . . ." or "Why don't you try such-and-such?"—that all comes from my own fear.

I think it's disrespectful of someone else's life process to assume that they are inadequate to their experience. It would be good to follow that back and see how I am simply projecting my own fear of inadequacy onto them. I truly cannot know about someone else's life.

Have I told you my image of cleaning the house? To me this is a more helpful attitude of mind: I have this house and it's dirty and I enjoy cleaning it. I would want you, as my guest, to be in the room that's already cleaned. I am offering the merit of that work to you for your enjoyment. Meanwhile, I'm going to be working on the rooms that are still dirty. I can know that you have your own work to do, your stuff to clean up, but that's yours, and it's not my concern. The contribution I can make is to clean up what's mine.

DENNIS: Within that, is there any hope that it also helps me clean up mine?

CHERI: No. I can't help you go down your path, I can't remove your obstacles. But I can avoid putting things in your way. So everything of mine that I take responsibility for along the way may make it easier for you. In the meditation hall, I can't influence anyone's sitting and I wouldn't want to, but I can be quiet. I can work at coming back to the present, I can avoid being a disruption. That's very different from saying, "I'm going to do this, and now your job is to do that."

RIC: In the example of the house, if someone hadn't told me to clean it, why would I?

CHERI: I clean mine because I want to.

RIC: Let's say I'm in a house and I see dirt on the floor, and there's a broom in the corner, and I sweep up the dirt. It's possible that someone would come and say, "That dirt was there for a good reason. How dare you remove it?"

CHERI: That's right. And then you might look at what was going on with you, and maybe what you would see was that you didn't really give a flying fig about that dirt, but you thought everybody would say, "Look at Ric, what a great guy, he cleaned up the house." Or maybe what you would see is, "I really enjoyed doing it and I hope it didn't interfere with anybody, and I hope if they want me to put it back, they'll ask me." And you never think about it again.

In this way I do most deeply vow to train myself.

6 Not to publish other people's faults

There are no victims or perpetrators

Key: Kindness

Prohibition: Not blaming or criticizing

Aspiration: To acknowledge responsibility
for everything in my life

Inspiration: *There are no victims or perpetrators*

CHERI: On my mind tonight are dark chocolate and white sugar. That's how I can tell the retreat is half over. Does anyone else experience that? Or have you all transcended craving? I just imagined someone publishing my faults, and I wonder where craving chocolate and sugar would be on that list.

JOHN: The word "fault" suggests imperfections, or that something could be another way. How are we to understand a precept that refers to something being other than the way it is?

CHERI: Well, I confess, that strikes me as well. This is the one precept that doesn't take projection into account.

Projection is attributing to others qualities in ourselves. Judgment, which always comes up in discussing the precepts, is simply projecting our own tendencies and concerns and fears and desires out onto something external.

We have this idea that it is wrong to judge others, but, in fact, seeing our projections and owning them is extremely useful in this process of getting to know ourselves. If I notice myself saying that Rodney is so-and-so, I can realize that I don't know anything about Rodney, but so-and-so is indeed true for *me*. Of course, we could all get together and say, "Yeah, but Rodney really is like that." But that just means we're all conditioned in the same way, and we all share that projection. If we asked Rodney, he could say he didn't see it that way at all. Or he could agree—in which case it's more confusing, because then we want to say, "See, we were right." But we still would not know anything about Rodney's experience, only about our own. So, it is helpful to put on hold the notion that we can know anything about anything except ourselves.

This precept can remind us that if we're honest, we seldom see anything anybody else is doing that we couldn't match to some degree.

Now, it is still true that this precept carefully followed, just at face value, is incredibly helpful. For instance, if I'm honest, I seldom see anything anybody else is doing that I couldn't match. The particulars might be different, but the process of it is much the same. So, it's helpful to be reminded to look right back here and examine what's going on with me. This precept can be that reminder.

GENE: Two of the precepts say not to do such-and-such "nor encourage others to do so." I'm wondering why they don't all say that.

CHERI: Especially with this precept, it might be helpful to add that on.

Here's something that happens a lot at the monastery, and probably here, too. At a silent retreat, somebody comes up and starts talking to you, and you know it's not the thing to be doing because we're in silence. From this perspective, your response is simply to bow and walk away. Even in the monastery people don't do that because they're afraid of being perceived as a goody-two-shoes. Yet doing anything else is encouraging someone in an unhelpful way. If you bow and walk off they might not react well, but they might also stop and think about it and get to a point of realizing how they were putting you in a miserable position because you came here not to talk. Of course, you want to get ready to be on the receiving end of that, too—when you think something is important and you need to tell somebody, and they bow and walk away. Then you can come back to that awareness of, "Whoops, thank you, that was helpful—painful but helpful."

PATTI: But out in the world, people don't usually understand when you do something like that. At work there are some people I talk to when they need to vent about something someone else has done, and we can focus it back to what this has to do with them. But other people are not going to find the idea of projection helpful.

CHERI: What is motivating *you* in this interaction? Bowing and walking off is not going to be acceptable, telling them about projection isn't helpful—what's going on here? Are you really concerned about them?

PATTI: No. I'm concerned about how I think I'm helping them.

CHERI: And are you also concerned about how you're being perceived by them?

PATTI: Yes. I work with these people every day so I don't want to irritate them, because that could make it uncomfortable for the rest of my time there.

CHERI: And so we just dig a deeper hole. But can you consider how you might respond from what's actually going on with you? It's worth considering how that might work.

JESSICA: Especially with gossip, breaking this precept might be an inappropriate way to reach out and not feel lonely. When I talk about other people, it's a way of trying to connect. And with some of the other precepts, too, I break them in an attempt to hold at bay that existential emptiness. So, some of this behavior arises because "I," egocentricity, is very lonely.

CHERI: And two "I"s can get together and reinforce one another. That's why it's so hard to stop somebody who is gossiping to you. At more lucid moments either of us might say, "No, gossiping is not the thing to do." Yet there we are engaged in it, and neither of us is able to call it off.

ELLEN: One thing that helps me at work is to avoid situations where gossip tends to happen. I'm much more likely to get caught up in it in a group. Not that it happens that much less with only one other person, but I can see it so much easier.

MARY: I've got a good reason to keep this precept, which is that if the notion of projection is correct, then I don't want to have my own faults out there for everyone to see.

CHERI: Again, the precepts help us look at how we are. The people we share this practice with, the sangha, also help us with that. In a group like this, we tell what we struggle with, what we stumble over. We compare notes, and pretty soon we realize we're all pretty much the same. We all do the same processes, we suffer with the same issues, so we can realize that maybe there's more to it than a right way to be and a wrong way to be.

We could just observe the ways we suffer and say, "This is the kind of thing egocentricity does," and then we could choose not to operate from that conditioning. I could see something in myself or in other people or I could simply read about it in the paper and say, "That's not something I want to do." Or I might see something in someone else that is causing suffering, then ask myself, what is the form of that that I do? How do I feel about myself when I do it? Or, if I am unable to see it in myself, what might I be suppressing to keep from doing it?

This is different from believing that someone is inherently flawed, that the behavior that causes suffering is who they really are. In fact, conditioned behavior is who they are not. Let's say the person in the car repair shop keeps putting tires on backwards. This doesn't mean that the person is bad, but because it's important to get the tires on right, we need to notice when they are put on wrong and to point that out so it can be done differently. Unfortunately, we have almost no experience of acknowledging that something doesn't work or is not a good way to be without tagging on "and you are a bad person" for doing this or being this way.

What is wrong? And who is responsible?

JACKIE: With this precept, I think about some scandals that have become public recently, and to me it's important to have the facts presented as to what people have done. Like Zen centers where teachers have abused their power.

CHERI: Only in Zen centers?

JACKIE: No, but I think one reason people didn't speak up when they knew what was going on was that they didn't want to publish faults. But I think a lot of damage was done. It's not necessary to speak up in a hateful or blaming way, but by stating that these actions have taken place, people can decide whether or not they want to be involved with these groups. I don't think I can take this precept if it means that

I don't speak up about sexual abuse if I'm aware of it. I think it would be wrong not to speak up.

CHERI: To believe that I can never say anything about any-body no matter what the circumstances—yes, that seems irresponsible. But I am bothered by the assumption that I should decide what other people should be informed about.

RIC: I agree with Jackie that there are things that are poten-tially harmful or dangerous, and it's hard to look at some-thing like that and conclude that there's no problem.

CHERI: But that's not what we're talking about here. We're talking about spiritual practice. We're not deciding how we should treat one another in order to create a society that's going to serve each of us in the manner we would prefer. We're talking about how to end suffering.

RIC: But these things happen in our daily lives.

CHERI: My daily life is not different from my spiritual practice.

RIC: Exactly.

CHERI: So I'm not going to have a different set of standards for my daily life than for my spiritual practice.

RIC: Right.

CHERI: Why do I still feel we're not quite in agreement on this?

RIC: It makes sense that I would ask those questions, trying to live in the world.

CHERI: Yes, there are lots of things in the world that are scary, if we want to view it that way. But to try to protect ourselves, to try to change externals in such a way that we will be safe and comfortable, seems to me dangerous, from a spiritual perspective.

GREG: When I first heard about a Buddhist teacher saying things that sounded like publishing people's faults, I struggled to see how it was possible to do that without breaking this precept. Finally it dawned on me that maybe the person who made the critical remark was just stating an observation instead of finding fault—maybe interpreting it as a fault was coming from me.

We saw a film at our Zen center about another Zen center, and at the time, there was a lot of concern about the teacher there. I was upset because it sounded like the people at our Zen center thought there was something wrong with that teacher for being alcoholic. The next night I told everybody what was wrong with *them* because of what they had said about the teacher. Then Cheri asked if I could see how I was doing what I said they were doing. And eventually I did see that.

The more I understand about projection, the easier it is when I see that a person did a crummy job or made a mistake or doesn't understand—any time there's that feeling of something wrong with somebody else—I immediately look to see how that's so in me. For example, in the past if I heard someone was a racist, I would take that to mean that he was a bad person. But now with that same information, I look to myself to see how someone could do things I think of as racist— how I myself do those things—rather than condemn that other person.

The longer I do this practice, the less willing I am to jump to conclusions about people. If one of the monks started showing up smelling like alcohol every day, I don't know what I'd do or say, but I'm not so willing to assume there's something wrong with that person. Or that there's something about what that person is doing that's going to hurt me. I'm suspicious of wanting to point fingers at people and feeling righteous, and thinking that you're not moral if you don't point the finger.

SARA: There's a little follow-up to that story about the alcoholic teacher, which I heard as pure gossip, so I'd like to relate it before I take this precept. It put this sort of thing in perspective for me. If I understood it right, the teacher's students decided he had a drinking problem, they put pressure on him to go into an alcoholic rehabilitation program, and when he came out somebody asked him what he'd learned. And he said he learned that Americans have strong feelings about alcohol.

CHERI: I hear more about this kind of thing than I want to, and my favorite response is my own. A woman was getting ready to leave our Zen center to move near the one Greg and Sara are referring to, and she wanted a group to sit with. I mentioned that Zen center, and she said, "Oh, no, you know about all the stuff that went on there." I said, "Look, here's the deal. Don't drink with them. Don't take drugs with them. Don't sleep with them. Just sit with them."

We all want to be protected against our own experience, but in terms of spiritual practice, that won't work. This person's faults [*pointing to self*] are plenty for me to deal with. If I could be protected against this person, if I could get some sort of guarantee against harm from myself, then I might be safe in the world.

In this way I do most deeply vow to train myself.

7

There are

Not to extol oneself and slander others

no winners or losers

Key: Humility

Prohibition: Not competing or coveting

Aspiration: To give my best effort and accept the results

Inspiration: *There are no winners or losers*

CHERI: Does not extolling oneself and slandering others seem the same as not publishing the faults of others?

MARY ELLEN: Both these precepts seem particularly related to inadequacy. So much of my life seems driven by the feeling of inadequacy, and I can either give in to that feeling, or I can try to prove it wrong by extolling myself. But it's just two sides of the same coin.

MARY: Inside my head, I can see clearly the absurdity of taking my own judgments seriously, because it's just flip-flopping between "Aren't you wonderful?" and "You're really awful," back and forth, back and forth. But when I see the same extolling and slandering as outside of me, I believe it: "That person really is better than I am," or, "I really am better than that person."

KAREN: For me, it's easier to catch myself on this one when my judgments are in response to someone else. But it goes on all the time, about everything.

CHERI: Yes, no, yes, no; better, worse, better, worse. The world of opposites. Duality.

ACKER: Of all the tapes I hear playing in my head, this one seems to be operating on fast-forward. At first, it's almost indiscernible, but when I stop and notice, there have been many times in the last few minutes that I've said "good, bad, good, bad," about myself or about another person, without being fully conscious of it. It's taking duality and separateness to its highest form—or its lowest form. Our need to establish how distinct we are from that next person is revealed in this high-speed, back-and-forth, continual reiteration.

CHERI: In fact, we can evaluate people and reject them without having been consciously aware of them. Ever notice that? In a crowd, for instance, we are capable of instantaneous judgments.

LINDA: I feel a little lost. Does "extolling" mean feeling food about yourself? Not to puff up the ego, not to feel too good about myself—that was hammered into me as a child, so it strikes a nerve. My inclination is to say, "Let's feel good about ourselves, and let's feel good about everybody else, too."

CHERI: I hope there is a way you can feel good about who you are, feel good about who everybody is, and sort of slide in between these issues, where there is just a genuine appreciation for everyone. If I'm just another person on a circle and I'm not taking myself personally anymore, I get a share of everything too, like everybody else—that sort of feeling.

LINDA: Somehow in this discussion I haven't heard it that way. It sounds to me more like people are being hard on themselves for feeling good about themselves.

GREG: It has a lot to do with the extol/slander duality. This precept works both ways, not to slander oneself and extol others as well as the way it's written. It doesn't make any difference whether I'm making myself better or making myself worse in comparison to others, it's the same process.

When we're right here fully present, we're just seeing who everybody is and enjoying that.

Something Cheri said for a long time before I got it was, "If you're going to like yourself, then like everybody. If you're going to dislike yourself, then dislike everybody." And if you do that, it's not so easy to keep up the duality of the self-and-other game. I think it's great to feel good about myself and feel good about everybody, but if I want to be a separate self, I can't do it that way. It just doesn't work: if I'm going to be good, someone else has to be bad, or if I'm going to be bad, someone else has to be good. It's not that the way to keep this precept is to put myself down or fail to appreciate myself. The precept is more a description of how I stay separate.

CHERI: Linda is pointing out that from a centered place, there's just a genuine appreciation. Any time we move away from that, we are in that back-and-forth, back-and-forth. But when we're right here being fully present to the moment, we're just seeing who everybody is and enjoying that.

CHERI: If I recognize that I have done something harmful, it is useful to stay with the disappointment of that—not getting into what a bad person I am, how I shouldn't have done it, making promises never to do it again, because all of that is simply an ego salvage system. But if I can allow myself to feel the hurt to my heart, there is nothing for conditioning to get hold of. It's possible to stay in that awareness and not be looking for some way out so I can forget what I did and begin to be lulled back to sleep. Of course, egocentricity will react against the awareness with doubt or fear or self-hate, but that is exactly what I'm watching for; I'll pay attention and see how it happens. Then, if I stay with the pain, conditioning will tell me, "This doesn't feel good." If I stay present, though, it does feel good—it feels alive in a way that is not possible when I'm stuck in conditioning, because when I am present, all the energy that is usurped by the ego salvage system is available to me.

It's easy to think that what we are trying to do is find the part in us that truly doesn't want to extol ourselves and slander others. But that doesn't work. The part in us who thinks that is simply the other side of the duality—the one who criticizes the part that does extol and slander, the one who points out what's wrong with us. Wouldn't the best thing be to go on and say whatever we say, but pay attention? We all know we do these things, so nothing changes except that we would add an effort to stop the self-punishment so we don't endlessly go around in these circles. Just say it, and pay attention. Look to see where it's coming from, how it feels, what goes on with it.

If I want to pursue this further, I might choose something somebody says to me that is hurtful, and consider, how do I do that to others? My project will be to observe over a month, or three months or six months, something in myself that I dislike in somebody else. Let's say a co-worker pointed out a mistake I made and did it with a smug, superior attitude that I really hate. I'd start by writing "smug and superior" on sticky notes, and I'd put them all around places I'm going to be, just to keep the subject of smug and superior on my mind. I may tell people close to me that I'm working on this issue, and please *not* to inform me of times in the past when I was smug and superior—that will simply make me defensive and keep me from seeing what I'm looking for.

Sometimes I'll do something and then I'll hear a voice in myself say, "Well, that qualifies as smug and superior." Other times there's simply a sense of knowing that the person I just spoke to might experience my delivery as smug and superior. So what is going on with me there? Am I unaware of certain mannerisms and styles of speech? Am I covering up self-consciousness, or am I afraid of how the person is going to respond, so that my language becomes sort of stilted in a way that might be misinterpreted? What exactly was motivating me right then? Many voices will comment on all this, but there will also be moments of clarity, when I actually see my smugness and superiority and how I am operating unconsciously out of my conditioning.

It may take a while to realize why I had such a strong reaction to the other person being smug and superior. But when I do see that in myself, it doesn't make me a "bad" person, it makes me a compassionate person. Because then I don't have to be exasperated and intolerant and blaming when somebody else behaves in a smug and superior way. I know exactly what it feels like to do it. Being present to it all, with nothing else going on, is the compassion, and the compassion allows for the clarity. Without the compassion, I may have the same insight, but it gets filtered into a conditioned response—"I had a really good reason . . . He did it first . . ."—and the insight is corrupted, internalized in the corrupted form, and added to the conditioned stew.

People often observe that it would be helpful to expand this precept to include the reverse: not to slander oneself and extol others. I suspect the slandering self and extolling others came first, and that extolling ourselves and slandering others arose as a defense.

Think of how it works in the conditioning process: as children, we are brought out of our own little world into the world of correct behavior. One of the first ways that happens is by instilling in us the sense of being watched by our parents. To children it's like magic: how do parents know what we do when they're not even in the same room? That initiates the process of us watching ourselves in the same way, to make sure we're not doing something "wrong" for which we will be punished. Then there comes the next element, which is God watching us. God doesn't even have to be in the house; God sees and hears and knows everything. At a certain age we learn that we can actually fool our parents; we can *think* something and our parents won't know about it. But God knows. So there's no escape; we feel as if we're being watched all the time. And, to avoid punishment, we end up trying to watch ourselves at a level that will outfox God.

It's quite a shift to go from that kind of self-consciousness to watching ourselves the way we do in this practice, which is with compassion. We can begin to identify with the compassion which is the inherent goodness of all that is. Most people project that compassion outward and conceptualize it as a deity, but it is available within ourselves—it's who we are. In Buddhism we talk about it as our true nature, our original or authentic self, which has been covered over with conditioning. The difficulty we struggle with is that because it was covered over so early, before we had the ability to conceptualize, it seems as if the conditioning is original. If we knew our inherent goodness first, none of these difficulties would exist. We would not suffer. We would know goodness as our true nature, we would understand how conditioning happened to us, we wouldn't take it personally, there would be no idea that we deserved to suffer because our deepest being is flawed, sinful.

The essence of this practice is discovering that inherent goodness, recognizing it as the deepest and truest in us, and from that experience we can embrace into compassion all the things that happen to us through conditioning. We sit in meditation to find that goodness, to let the spaces between the conditioning become larger so we can see that compassionate clarity around us. We feel it, we recognize it in ourselves, we recognize it in the rest of life, we can sense that we move within it, it's what's there when everything else stops. It is crucial to make that shift.

Because we are so conditioned to believe that we are inherently bad, this approach is extremely threatening. Egocentricity responds with, "So, you're just going to drop all the rules? You're going to let people do whatever they want to do? With no controls, no restraints, they will sink into their evil nature." That is extremely frightening, which is why it's essential to prove to ourselves that our inherent nature is goodness. Then there's no fear. Once we know who we are, there's no fear that we will be bad. To do something bad, we would have to leave who we are, and we have no interest in that, when what we are is compassionate and joyful and good and loving and kind and generous.

ELLEN: Today walking around in the mist I've been experiencing these waves of emotion, and feeling blissful and special in a centered kind of way. Then seeing another person would trigger a response of wanting to feel special because that person thinks certain things about me. So, that specialness I had just been feeling wasn't enough. Both these precepts seem to refer to situations with other people in which I'm trying to give my ego a shot in the arm. But when I'm not doing that, I can just take my own place in the circle.

CHERI: I would suggest that everyone take a walk up the

mountain because it's clearly the happening place. I was up there myself in the mist and the fog, and watching how I would be totally blissful and then I would start making comparisons. There's special, and then there's special. When you're caught in your conditioning, there's a limited amount of specialness. But if you're centered, specialness is something that everyone can have; there's plenty, so everybody can be equally special.

In this way I do most deeply vow to train myself.

8 Not to be avaricious in bestowal of the teachings

Key:	Piety
Prohibition:	Not apostatizing or denying spiritual responsibility
Aspiration:	To live an openly spiritual life
Inspiration:	*There is nothing in my life that is not part of my spiritual training*

PATTI: I think of this as the opposite of the second precept: instead of not taking that which is not given, not withholding that which is to be given.

KAREN: This one can apply to people asking me why I wear the beads [given in the precepts ceremony], when I have to take a few breaths and figure out what I want to say. Sometimes the impulse is to lecture, or sometimes an answer comes from extolling myself. But this precept makes me stop and say, "What do I want to share about this? What am I being asked? And how do I want to respond to that right now?"

CHERI: So you're looking at it in terms of what your motivation is, what's in this for your practice, as well as what another person might be able to relate to?

KAREN: Yes. It includes what's going on with me as well as what they're asking, and in light of that, what to say. And I find that very difficult sometimes.

RODNEY: There seems to be a contradiction in that we say we are training ourselves, yet "bestowal of the teachings" implies another realm, a realm of involvement with others.

MARY: I don't see a conflict there. Talking with somebody about a process I've learned can make it clearer for me. My willingness to be engaged with another person in this way seems to be a part of my training, because often the first time I understand something is when I hear it from my own mouth, in response to somebody else.

RIC: I also thought about what "avaricious" might mean. I can be very identified with a particular body of knowledge or set of experiences—say, as a person who knows a lot about AIDS or a person who works in the field of domestic violence. I love to share my knowledge, to feel that this is who I am. But I see my avarice in that I want to be thought of as having something other people don't have, rather than acknowledging that there are these teachings, and they are passed along, and they don't belong to anybody.

JESSICA: After I'd been doing this practice for a couple of years, I thought it would be nice to share it, so I organized a meditation group through the Unitarian Fellowship where I live. I told people how to meditate, and we listen to tapes, and there is a little discussion. If people ask me a specific question, I try to answer it, and I'll give people addresses of meditation centers, and I'll lend tapes. But as I've continued, I've been less willing to give out knowledge, because I'm not sure I have it; I've become less certain. Not that I doubt the path, but I doubt myself. If I don't know what I'm doing, I figure, it's better not to do very much.

CHERI: You're probably in a perfect place to bestow teachings, if you will, because what you'll be saying to people is, "This is what I've experienced, and if you meditate, you'll have your own experience of it." All we're ever doing is giving people the encouragement to meditate until they have the understanding for themselves, rather than telling them what is the truth. We are way more dangerous when we think we know everything than when we know nothing.

Practicing the precepts

GREG: To me, the point of this practice is not to avoid "breaking" the precepts. In fact, the more I pay attention to my experience in terms of the precepts, the more I see that I break them. Instead, I think of the process as a kind of science, and I'm a scientist—a "Gregologist"—and the precepts are tools to study how this character works. With that approach, I see it all as very interesting. Otherwise, it could be horrible.

CHERI: The quickest way to end your spiritual training is to use what you see against yourself, because if you beat yourself up every time you see something about yourself, being an intelligent person, pretty soon you're going to stop seeing things. We're not trying to "keep" the precepts in any way that would lead to feeling that if we didn't keep one, we were bad or did something wrong. That's missing the point.

And it's not as if I have to worry about what you're doing, or you have to worry about what I'm doing. It's all internal: I watch my conditioned responses and see if they are in line with the deepest desire of my heart.

So, how do you do that? For example, it's important not to turn to how you *feel* to know how you *are*. If you quit smoking after twenty years, you may feel like garbage, but that doesn't mean you're not doing the right thing. Or if you have difficulty asking your partner for time to meditate, you might feel awful when you go ahead and do it, but that's not an indication that there's anything wrong with it. On the other hand, you might have three drinks and feel great, and that's not necessarily an indication that that's a good thing. So we look toward something else. What is that?

KAREN: There's a certain sense I equate with being centered. It's more like a feeling than anything else.

CHERI: But it doesn't necessarily mean that you're happy or peaceful?

KAREN: No, or that all the debates are figured out.

GREG: I would say that it's not necessarily feeling happy or peaceful, but there is a sense of underlying happiness and peace that is not disturbed by things that are going on. I may be in pain and feel unhappy and be upset, but underneath all that, there's a way in which everything is fine.

AURELIA: I step back from the present and think about the consequences of what's going on—not just the here and now but the broader view, aside from my immediate desires. And that sometimes makes me behave differently.

DENNIS: When I think of how these precepts came about, it seems to me that people must have looked at the Buddha and asked, "What is he doing?" Then they came up with these precepts that describe what they understood the Buddha to be doing, with the idea that if they tried to do these things, they could also be like that. But I think it has to be the other way around: instead of adding these precepts onto my life, they have to come from within. I think that an enlightened person—even myself, when I am centered—would just *be* these things. The external expression would happen naturally, without effort.

In spiritual practice it is important to drop the assumption that we understand.

With the first precept, I considered whether there are times when not killing doesn't apply. For example, is there a way of killing in need? Like Eskimos, where their whole ecosystem is just animals and them. Is there a way they could kill that actually opens their hearts when it happens?

CHERI: Of course, I could never answer a question about their experience. But the direction of your questioning is helpful, because it suggests that, "I can't know that, and therefore it's not for me to make a decision about it," rather than, "They are wrong, so there's an entire group of people with big bad karma."

As we do spiritual practice, we want to remember to find the willingness to drop the assumption that we understand. To have faith that as we proceed, as we continue to sit and practice, we will see more. What appears one way at a certain point of understanding may appear completely different at another point.

And we want to remember that we are doing this entirely by choice, as a way of looking after our own spiritual well-being.

MELINDA: There are a couple of analogies I find useful in clarifying how the precepts are to be used for our benefit. The first is training wheels. The precepts help keep us upright and on the path and moving along as we enter into practice and learn to live the practice. As we internalize the precepts, just having them register silently in our minds offers a stabilizing effect. Say, for instance, that I am angry. "Not to be angry" gets my attention. It makes me look at what is going on, it brings me into the present moment. It may keep me from careening into rage or from acting out of anger. It reminds me that I am doing spiritual practice, and I need to pay attention.

The second analogy is freeway "blot-dots," the little round bumps that line highways and alert drivers to when a double line is crossed, which means a danger zone is entered. The precepts wake us up when we wander off into unconsciousness. As I am criticizing someone, "Not to publish other people's faults" whispers at the back of my mind. Maybe I can stop what I'm doing, maybe not, but at least I notice it, I become aware. No punishment, nothing wrong, simply a reminder that I have left the middle way and have been pulled into conditioning. It can be very subtle, no more than a little twitch of discomfort or disharmony, a sense that something isn't quite right.

I remember someone pointing out that the precepts were written for egocentricity, because only ego needs training wheels and blot-dots as reminders to drop the conditioned responses and return to the present moment. From the present, no reminders are needed, because the precepts are the way life lives when it is unobscured by ego.

JAN: I have thought about the precepts almost entirely in terms of how my acts affect other people, and I'm realizing that I need to learn how not to be harmful to myself. In just the days I've been here, I see so many ways I can be kind to myself that I neglect in my daily life. I think if I could cultivate kindness with myself, I would naturally be kind to others.

CHRIS: I find that I can get to all the other precepts through the first one. If I violate any of them, it's harming something or someone.

CHERI: Are we still loosely associated with "not to be avaricious in bestowal of the teachings?"

GREG: If we go on the assumption that they're all the same precept.

DENNIS: I've been finding that for me they are all the same precept. There's a sense when I go in one direction that I'm going against the precept, and by paying attention to that and honoring that sense, I can stay within the guidelines. That's what I keep trying to focus on, whatever that sense is within myself. There can be a feeling of harmfulness associated with doing something, a lack of freedom, as if something closes down. Then when I act another way or from another intent, there's an opening to life. For me, that's how it becomes all the same precept, essentially.

CHERI: Different facets of the same jewel, perhaps.

In this way I do most deeply vow to train myself.

9 Not to be angry

Key: Acceptance

Prohibition: Not to rage, resent, or seek revenge

Aspiration: To see everything as an opportunity

Inspiration: *There are no mistakes*

RIC: I am feeling more committed around the essence of all this, but I'm still struggling with some of the specifics. When I think of the one on anger, I can say, "What a wonderful opportunity; that is a big issue for me, yes, indeed." But whether I'm going to agree with the letter of "Do not be angry," I don't know.

CHERI: It doesn't say that. It says, "Not to be angry."

RIC: What's the difference?

CHERI: To me, "not to be angry" speaks to a state, which is very different from "never have an angry impulse arise."

RIC: So, one is a commandment and—

CHERI: —the other is a process dealing with what anger is. Where does it come from? What does it mean? How does it happen?

RIC: I led an anger management workshop at an AIDS clinic, and within about fifteen minutes two or three of the guys said, "Are you telling us not to feel this? Because anger is the one thing that is motivating us. That's what's giving us energy, that's what's helping us keep alive. Don't even hint that that should be taken away." Maybe they were too caught up in the unfairness of something happening to them that shouldn't happen to anybody, but who am I to tell them not to be angry?

If I want to look at what keeps me from being fully present, anger is a big one.

CHERI: I would never tell anyone not to be angry. I take this precept to work with in my own spiritual training. If I want to look at what keeps me from being fully present, anger is a big one.

RIC: You don't see it as one more thing that arises, and you watch it and let it go, just like any other emotion?

CHERI: The precept doesn't say to suppress anger. It's the same for this one as for the others. With the precept not to lead a harmful life, I look at my understanding of what harmful means and how that works in my experience, and I pay attention to what happens with me around that issue.

RIC: There's no precept that says not to be sad, not to be hurt, not to be afraid. Why "not to be angry?"

MIRIAM: I think anger points a finger, and that blaming takes responsibility away from yourself.

PATTI: It definitely takes me away from myself. If I sit with any anger long enough, I find that it comes from something quite different underneath it, usually fear. So, "not to be angry"— would that mean not to be afraid?

CHERI: Or not to cover up your fear with anger?

PATTI: Something else I'm aware of is how anger ties into intoxication. Self-righteous anger can be like a drug for me; it completely takes me out of the experience of fear or pain or whatever is underneath it. It's actually mood-altering, it's a weird high. It's different from experiencing anger, expressing anger, and not turning it against someone else. When it turns into self-righteousness, it violates other precepts.

GENE: "Not to be angry" suggests to me not an emotion but a state of mind in which someone is always angry and just waiting for a provocation to let it out. I'm not understanding this to say do not get angry; anger can be mobilizing if you're in a bad situation and you finally say to yourself, "I deserve better than this and I'm going to change it." If it takes building up a head of steam to do that, maybe that's appropriate—as opposed to staying in that state all the time waiting for something to happen so you can explode.

RIC: I know it's no fun to be around someone who is angry all the time, but I am questioning whether there is any other way of getting things done, in cases like AIDS work.

CHERI: To me, the idea that I have to be angry in order to accomplish something is a false assumption. I need to be willing to stay with something when there isn't that adrenaline rush pushing me on to whatever it is.

With all the precepts, I recommend continuing the behavior for as long as you can, paying attention to it, rather than saying, "Under these circumstances, I can have a drink and it's okay," or, "Under these circumstances, I can get angry and it's okay." If what we're talking about is being present—being right here, versus being out there—what advantage is it to us to try to come up with a situation in which it's all right to be out there?

RIC: It sounds like it's all right to feel anything. So why isn't it all right to feel angry?

CHERI: It is.

RIC: You just said something different, I think.

CHERI: You can do anything you want. Nobody is saying you should or should not do anything. It's just that if you want to be right here—fully present, centered—then pursuing anger is not going to do that for you.

GREG: For me, part of the problem is *not* feeling anger itself, but the righteousness and utter separateness and other stuff I make up when I'm in that state. And focusing on that, I miss what's actually going on—all the harm anger causes in the body, all the thought connections that get made up about another person and the situation. I'm ignoring so much when I'm angry. It cuts me off from the whole rest of the universe.

RIC: I agree about the self-righteous part. I can agree to look at anger in my life, even to single it out as something especially important to watch, because it has gotten me in trouble. But I'm having a hard time about this precept selecting anger out of all the emotions and the wording "not to be angry."

CHERI: There's an awful lot of emotion behind this, Ric. It might be good to sit with it.

RIC: I agree that this is a major issue in my life, and I'll sit with it and look at it—and I may not be ready to take the precepts.

CHERI: You could take the precept not to lead a harmful life knowing full well that you do lead a harmful life, but that you're working on that. You understand that leading a harmful life causes you to suffer, and you want to end suffering, so you don't have a problem with taking that precept. In the same way, to see that anger leads toward suffering . . .

RIC: No, I don't see that yet. I see that pursuing anger, indulging it—that is different. Maybe it sounds like rationalizing, but I don't agree that allowing myself to feel that emotion gets me into trouble. In fact, not to be angry sounds like it would get me into greater trouble.

CHERI: Once again, Ric, the precept does not say to suppress anger. It's about moving toward a time in your life when you're not coming from a state of anger.

MELINDA: It's not saying, "Don't feel." It's saying not to *be* angry. For me part of the understanding is that being angry puts it onto somebody else, which is doing harm—battering someone else with my cursing or violence or whatever. But there's nothing about not feeling angry. Certainly you're going to feel anger; we're all going to feel anger. As I understand it, there's no "should." And one of the most important things about all the precepts is that they're not to be ways of punishing ourselves—they're to help us pay attention.

GENE: One of the problems I see with getting angry about things is that it shifts my attention away from my responsibility to take care of myself. For instance, I can look at my childhood and my family and be angry because they did not give me things I wanted. I can come up with all sorts of reasons why I would be justified in being angry about that. But at some point I've got to move on. My life isn't going to get any better as long as I'm focused on blaming somebody else for where I am, regardless of how justified I might feel about it. So that to me is one of the issues with anger—as long as you stay with the anger, you're not taking responsibility, and you're not improving your situation.

JESSICA: I have two different experiences of anger. I can get worked up into a steam with a lot of dialog going on, and five minutes later I wake up and realize I just told myself the same angry tale I've told myself innumerable other times, just with the names changed. But when I am sitting and more centered and paying attention to what's going on, I've had the experience of feeling what I call anger come and go and be replaced by fear or sadness. And these are very different experiences.

CHERI: Then it's just sensations arising. And at that point, you could label them anything, or nothing. They're simply sensations; you're just watching your conditioning arise.

RIC: So, Jessica, given that a whole lot of sensations arise and some of them feel like anger, do you have difficulty with this precept?

JESSICA: I'm not sure. It's clear to me that if I'm acting from anger, I'm harming myself, and that that is not compassionate. But I need to look at it more.

PATTI: For me, it's helpful not only to consider where anger comes from but to consider the other precepts, too. In those rare moments when I'm really clear, and I can see that there are no faults in other people and that there is no blame and there are no mistakes, then anger isn't possible.

CHERI: Anger almost has to assume that something is wrong.

GREG: Anger makes me feel real. It's one of the ways I know I exist. I like that experience of being overwhelmed. Anger is just something I can't do anything about, it's so big and it makes me feel so powerful. But, everything I do while I'm identified with that anger, I can use against myself. I can build up all this evidence of my guilt for that little bit of the splendid intoxication of being overwhelmed by anger.

CHERI: Anger is my field of expertise. At one point when I was in the monastery, my teacher said, "Do you think you're going to be able to let go of your anger in order to do this practice? Because you can have one or the other, this practice or your anger. Which are you going to choose?" So I knew I had to get to the bottom of it, and fast.

Whenever anger arose, I would be right there scrutinizing it. It got so that I could tell the very first sensation at the onset of an angry reaction. As several of you have mentioned, there's always something under anger. Eventually I could see how somebody would say something to me, I would feel pain, then I would move straight into rage. For a long time I wasn't aware of the pain part, because that's exactly why I got angry—in order to miss the pain. But as I watched more carefully, I could see it.

Suppressing anger was not an option for me; I would actively seek it out. I was studying, and I needed new specimens all the time to put under the microscope so I could watch and see how it happened.

RIC: Before you did the work that you're talking about, were you as committed to that precept as you were to the others? Had you already taken all the precepts?

CHERI: I certainly knew that not being angry was a precept of Buddhism, and I knew why. I had no doubt about the extent to which anger is harmful: it had ruined my entire life.

If we just think about the world situation, isn't it hard to imagine having a war if there were no anger? The other emotions simply don't seem as destructive. People could be very sad or very frightened and it wouldn't result in war. But people being very angry seems quickly to escalate into hostilities.

GREG: When you consider its consequences, anger is different from the other emotions in almost a quantitative way. How much harm am I likely to cause if I'm overwhelmed by sadness? Not much. How much harm am I likely to cause when I'm overwhelmed by anger? An awful lot.

RIC: I'm still stuck.

CHERI: We're trying hard to talk you through it . . .

RIC: And I appreciate it. But there are so many folks—clients and friends—whose journeys seem to include a phase when they need to be angry a lot, especially people with a history of abuse. They've turned it inward for a long time, and then there's a time when the rage comes out. I've found it helpful to encourage people to express their rage, because it empowers them and they feel much lighter and freer.

CHERI: My take on it is this: if you're angry, get into it and get through it. Having lived with my own anger, I know its destructiveness, and so I want to get to the point of understanding where that comes from, how I react to that, the conditioning around it, to see what I'm really experiencing. And that process moves me through it, to the other side.

RIC: You could say that about all the emotions.

CHERI: Yes, but anger is the one that is so destructive.

RIC: People keep saying that, and yet depression kills an awful lot of people—any emotion to an extreme . . . . I'm sorry. I know I'm pushing this hard, but it just doesn't make sense to me.

CHERI: Ric, the important thing is to look. Not just while you're here, but in your life to have the experience and see what happens and what you learn from that. You may conclude that you want to be angry for the rest of your life, and that would be okay.

RIC: Or I might conclude that I want to be free to be whatever I feel, including angry.

CHERI: I would encourage you to consider that that's no different from egocentricity wanting anything else, so I hope you'll keep looking. I hope we all keep looking at this precept and all the rest of them.

Difficulty as opportunity

RODNEY: Buddhism is criticized for being passive, for not reaching out in a more social, outgoing way in concern for others. Our efforts are primarily introspective: we work on ourselves. I've heard you explain this very well, but when I've tried to explain it to somebody else I failed to make it clear.

CHERI: If you have to choose between cleaning up your own act and trying to talk somebody else into cleaning up theirs, it would be very helpful to clean up your own act first. That is not to say don't be involved, just don't lose your focus. Don't think that changing something out there is going to make a difference for you.

At the very deepest place that I can look—which is not to be confused with truth on the matter—I cannot see a place in Buddhism for social activism. Because that has to be based on the assumption that there is something wrong, that something needs to be done.

As an individual, I may be particularly moved by the plight of the orphans in Uganda, and I may choose to spend my life working with them, but that is vastly different from something needing to be done about a problem.

RODNEY: One thing you've said that is so meaningful to me in addressing separateness is that there is a mode of mind we attain when we are here, centered in the present moment, and that is nondual. Anything away from here—past or future or whatever dimension, anything outside of the moment—leaves that mode of nonduality and goes into duality, which creates separateness. I find that very useful to remember.

CHERI: Here, centered in the moment, there are no problems.

RODNEY: Because there is no "I," there is no one to have a problem. From out there, away from center, everything is a problem. That's why to me the only thing we can really offer to anyone else is our own centeredness. People often ask, "Then what would stop you from leading a completely self-indulgent life?" Isn't that the fear behind the resistance to this? Isn't that why people look at Buddhism and say, "All those people do is work on themselves—and where does this leave the rest of society?" But I consider that the life I try to live is one of service. Knowing that being fully present ends all suffering and dissolves all problems doesn't inspire me to just drift off and do nothing. It inspires me to want to assist other people, to the degree I am able, in that same awareness.

RIC: I often get angry about this point—because I still see that there are problems. Everything you say makes sense, and yet being centered is not going to stop AIDS.

CHERI: It's not going to stop hunger or racism or war or AIDS, but neither is hating all those things and *not* being at one with all that is.

RIC: I don't quite buy that, because I've seen people who are very obsessed and angry, and as a consequence things do happen, the medical establishment does . . .

CHERI: Okay, Ric, now you're going to have an opportunity to take anger to a new level. People who are angry and obsessed about AIDS are angry and obsessed either because they have AIDS or people they care about have AIDS. They are not obsessed about it when it does not pertain to their lives. People who have somebody die of cancer get obsessed about cancer. People who love animals are obsessed about animals. There's no mystery about this. We get fired up about the things that directly threaten us, and we want something to change about that. It's human nature.

MIRIAM: One could be fired up about justice in general.

CHERI: One could, and I would say there's a person who probably feels good fired up. But I'm not convinced that they're necessarily accomplishing anything. All I'm putting forth is encouragement to look and see if coming from center has the effect that you think it will. Look into the assumption that there's no point in trying to do anything you consider good unless you're upset, angry, and personally identified.

RIC: Or unless I think there's a problem. I agree that I might be more effective, the calmer and more centered I am, but I still think there's a problem.

CHERI: You can *care* without having something be *wrong.* Caring is not a response to something being wrong. As your heart opens, you become more aware of people who are dying of all kinds of illnesses and diseases, people who are dying alone, so maybe you're moved to want to start a hospice program, or learn massage so you can offer massage to sick people whom other people may not want to touch. But none of that has to come from hatred of what is, or hatred of other people because of what is.

RIC: Not to beat a dead horse, but—well, it's possible that I'll continue to struggle with this for a while. Right now I'm realizing that it's not an all-or-nothing thing. In some moments I am carried away and become hard to be around and obsessed and driven, but at other times I do find this place that is centered, and at those moments, it's a lot easier for a group of us to be working along together. So I don't see that the goal is to stop being angry or stop seeing AIDS as a problem. It's the moment-by-moment thing, that in the midst of it all, I can find moments of centering and calm. And then it doesn't seem like such a problem. In fact, it seems like an opportunity.

CHERI: We are conditioned to believe that for life to continue, we have to make it happen, we have to make sure that things get done and in a particular way. But if I'm just dissolved into it, life happens, and it's not me. If I trust that life is adequate to living, there is nothing to get worked up about.

One of the things I like best about Zen practice is that I'm not required to believe that anything bad is going to happen to me. There's tremendous freedom in that. So, if my heart's desire is to end suffering, I might as well get on with finding out what happens when I simply respond in the moment. If I am concerned that I'll be insensitive or selfish or indulgent or cruel or whatever it is, rather than living my life in fear and hesitation, it's important to consider that I might not be those things—and then find out. If my whole life is contracted because I am afraid that I won't do the right thing, then, for me personally, the price that I am paying is too great. Being "good" by whatever standards is not enough of a payback for a life not lived.

If I am going to observe my anger, I would not want to involve other people in that. Yet it is inevitable; we involve other people all the time. In living a small, contracted, frightened, closed-off life, I am certainly affecting other people. Again, the fear is that I will be bad, but once we know that we are not bad, there is no danger in involving other people. I'm not suggesting that we leap out there and indulge in our conditioned behavior patterns. I am suggesting the opposite: that we be who we truly are in each moment and see if that is someone we need to keep a leash on.

There are three ways we can be with a behavior we're concerned about. We can be unconscious. We can be conscious and trying to alter the behavior by suppressing or denying it. Or, which I find most helpful, we can consciously allow the behavior, observing it as it happens and seeing the conditioning involved. We are not the conditioning, but we have a front row seat for watching it.

RIC: I've been working hard with all this, and it's been a lot of fun, actually. I've written pages and pages and pages stating my case, and I looked at that for what it is. And I've been feeling a huge wave of gratitude for the fact that I could struggle here with this, and we can all struggle together.

Last night I had a sort of gratitude dream. In it there was a spiritual teacher who said, "Thank you so much, Ric, for pointing out your struggle with the precept about anger. That precept is wrong. I've been waiting for the one person who had enough insight to notice it." *[laughter]*

I still don't know where this will end up, but I've been feeling a little more distance from it. And I see how I was acting out exactly what that precept is about and some of the consequences of that: how much longer it took for me to get centered afterwards, and something that felt like churning energy around me, which was unpleasant. So it was a good chance to see what happens when you struggle with a precept and violate it and get caught up in that.

When I can find compassion for myself, I can always find it for someone else.

CHERI: The value in that process is that it brings us back to compassion. When I can find compassion for myself in that kind of struggle, I can always find it for someone else. When I can't seem to let go, and I flail around until some miracle happens and then I move through it, I can realize that other people probably experience the same thing.

In this way I do most deeply vow to train myself.

10 Not to speak ill of this religion or any other

There is
nothing
in anyone else's life
that is not appropriate
to their spiritual
training

Key: Tolerance

Prohibition: Not persecuting others
or assuming spiritual authority

Aspiration: To encourage others to lead
a spiritual life, in their own way

Inspiration: *There is nothing in anyone else's life*
that is not appropriate to their
spiritual training

CHERI: This is one of my favorite precepts: "Not to speak ill of this religion or any other." Because I'm in the religion business, people sometimes try to lure me into conversations in which there is an opportunity to bad-mouth other religions.

Why bother with what's wrong about a religion? Why not just take the parts that work?

And since this is a predominantly Christian culture, Christianity is a good target.

But why bother with what's wrong about a religion? Why not just take the parts that work? Love one another. That's good; that seems to be what Jesus was talking about. I can't find anything to argue with in that.

People can get very worked up over what they perceive as flaws in a religion. It's as if their whole spiritual future hangs in the balance over the possibility of an inconsistency somewhere. "Is there some inconsistency in Buddhist teachings? If there is, I'm out of here." Because if we find something wrong, we can justify not doing this practice. Need I point out that this is a strategy of egocentricity?

ELIZABETH: I've never thought of what we do here as religious. It's a practice to me, but you talk about being in the religion business . . .

CHERI: Whenever someone says, "It's not religion, it's spiritual," I start having images of crystals and pyramids and digging a lot of wells about a foot deep. Religion doesn't bother me. I like religion.

CHRIS: It seems to me that you could do this practice within any religion.

SARA: How could you do it within a religion that required you to profess belief in something?

CHERI: Phyllis, our Catholic nun who is also a Zen monk, practices Buddhism within Christianity with no conflict at all. In fact, she and I recently instructed the Sisters of Notre Dame in this practice, and they're quite enthusiastic about it.

SARA: Don't they have to ignore some of their teachings to do this practice?

ACKER: If you went to another religion as a practitioner of Zen, you'd just be open to it all, wouldn't you? Not reject it or accept it, but just observe it.

SARA: My point is that some religions require you to accept their beliefs. That seems antithetical to what we're pursuing here.

CHERI: In the same way that last night Ric could be wherever he was with the process of anger, someone could be wherever they were in regard to religion.

One of the things I like best about this precept is the reminder that if I am following my spiritual practice, I won't have anything ill to say about anyone else. If I do, that's a sign for me that something within my practice needs attention.

MELINDA: Doesn't "ever-expanding faith" in the Daily Recollection imply belief?

CHERI: I think of belief as something fixed that I can refer back to or apply to something, whereas for me faith is akin to trust. I trust that nothing too terrible can happen to me. It's not that I believe that; there's just a sense of that being so.

MELINDA: For me, faith is tied in with giving myself permission to be a religious person. I've had to work toward finding the willingness to have faith, to trust that there is a realness to things spiritual, to allow myself to be a religious person, or anything other than the atheist I was raised as.

SARA: It's also hard for me to allow myself to be involved in something like this, and I've been able to do it precisely because I'm not expected to believe anything.

CHERI: This is how my teacher came to Buddhism. In a class he was taking on world religions, the instructor listed one word to describe each of the major spiritual traditions, and for Zen the word was "intelligent." My teacher had been brought up in a rather rigid and conventional religion, and he couldn't imagine applying the word "intelligent" to a religion. That fascinated him, and that's how he came to pursue Zen.

ACKER: But I think it would be good to find an attitude of compassion and acceptance toward the many people for whom conventional religion is helpful and reasonable.

CHERI: Absolutely, and I would imagine that after studying Zen, my teacher could have a greater appreciation for the religion he was brought up in.

JOHN: I've found that, too. It's been twenty years since I left the religion I was raised in, which was mainstream Methodist. I kind of slid through Unitarianism, where you don't have to believe anything, then got interested in Buddhism. But two summers ago, the church I belonged to growing up, where my sister still sings in the choir, asked me to come sing in the choir, because I used to and they were short of men.

I agreed to do it, but it took a lot of mental gymnastics. For example, I figured it was okay to sing Christian words, because if there was music with them, it wasn't the same as just saying them. And when it came time for the Apostle's Creed and the Lord's Prayer, I kind of mumbled and said every third word. I was worried about hypocrisy. But I enjoyed the singing and eventually the ritual and the ceremony as well, and the people I'd grown up with, people I liked. I ended up staying in the choir through Christmas. Then I started back again this summer and have become more and more comfortable.

On communion Sunday, which is every other month or so, I'd find some excuse not to be there, or I'd leave early. But two Sundays ago I took my first communion in twenty years, and it felt okay. I'm not sure I can explain how or why, because I certainly don't believe in much of it in a literal sense. Maybe I'm reinterpreting it all to suit me, but it doesn't feel hypocritical anymore. I can participate pretty fully and not feel in conflict with this practice.

JESSICA: I have another perspective on this. John is my husband, and I'm somewhat threatened by his going to church because I'm Jewish, and the folks those Christian inquisitors were burning were my ancestors. I think it's very hard being a non-Christian in a Christian culture, especially if there are no support systems. I don't go around speaking ill of Christianity, but I do feel a fear of it. My early experience was not that it is a loving and embracing religion, but that it was used against me personally.

CHERI: There is that old childhood desire and expectation that someone else will be the way they should be so that we will have a model, and the hope that we can be the way we know we should be. Religions often disappoint us in this respect.

Pointing out everyone else's prejudices is never going to lead to a lack of prejudice.

I would encourage all of us to cut out the middleman. Just do it yourself. If you want the world to be without prejudice, then be without prejudice yourself. Pointing out everyone else's prejudices is never going to lead to a lack of prejudice. I'm not suggesting that in this moment all prejudice is going to fall away from you and that will be the end of it. But I am suggesting that as long as we look for examples of how people are doing it wrong, we're going to find examples of how people are doing it wrong.

Now, there's somebody in you who's been traumatized by something related to this. Rather than leave her forever with a child's view of life, not understanding what happened, stuck in that pain and anger, you can help her move through it, help her gain a perspective that will allow her to let go of all that stuff she's carrying and make it easier for her to function in the world.

There are parallels between this precept and "not to be angry." In getting to know my anger, I may go through a process of relating to it in many different ways before I can simply allow the energy to go through my body without needing to label it or have a particular reaction to it. I may scream and swear and break things. In the same way with "not to speak ill of this religion or any other," a lot of speaking ill may need to come out as I am seeing what that is all about, although I don't have to involve anybody else in it. And there will be times when I become totally identified with my beliefs about it. I may have gotten to the point of writing it all down in a letter addressed to Pope, Vatican, Rome, and I may be looking up the zip code before I realize that I don't want to actually send all that to anybody—and it may take everything I have not to.

If we haven't resolved our problems with a religion we were involved in previously, we can be certain that we will repeat the whole process with this one. It's the same as in relationships: if we leave one relationship before we've seen what we did and how that worked and the suffering it caused, it will all be played out again in the next relationship.

If I'm concerned about intolerance for other people's beliefs, I've got to do the work to know how that happens within myself. Then I don't have to go around saying, "Why are people intolerant?" I know why—because they're conditioned to be that way, and they don't know any other way to be. Also, if anyone should ever ask, I have some ideas about how not to be that way.

JACKIE: This whole process of spiritual practice for me has been letting go of that delusion that there are perfect people out there somewhere and that I can become one of them. It's giving up a lot of fairy tales and fantasies and the illusion that anything other than the present is better than what's here. All that stuff that goes on in my mind—if I had a horse, I'd be happier, or maybe what I need is a dog; or if I read more spiritual books, I'd be a holier person. I'm amazed at how I still hold on to believing that somehow there's something else that will take care of me.

I've tried a lot of things, and with each one, I'm convinced that other people should try the latest thing I'm trying. But it doesn't last. Right now I'm struggling with the awareness that I have persisted with this particular path longer than any of the others, for about five years (which is also the longest I've ever been in a relationship), and I feel myself being resistant. I'm just going through the motions now; I don't seem to be able to do this practice whole-heartedly. Part of me just won't open up, and I keep finding reasons why it's ridiculous to go on with this. In the past, my tendency would always be to move on to something else at this point.

CHERI: And what a wonderful place to be: to work and work and work until you get to the point of seeing that. Not thinking, "Uh-oh, I need to get out of here and go pursue the real thing," or, "What is wrong with me that I can't just open up to something and fully commit my life to it?" But instead to just say, "Ah, here's my resistance. This is the thing to sit still with now, this is the thing to be with now."

SARA: This whole idea of religion is so difficult for me. Last night I lay awake with my mind racing, defending my right to speak ill of religion. I went through a list of what is wrong with each one. Basically, all religions are unacceptable except Buddhism, and within Buddhism, only one strand is free of various taints—superstition and so on—and that of course is Zen. But I couldn't go for Rinzai; it has to be Soto.

Of course there are many Soto Zen teachers I couldn't relate to: Cheri is really the only one I can imagine as my teacher. And even Cheri can be unreasonable . . . . Then I saw that in defending my right to find fault and reject, I had thrown away everything.

CHERI: Except your own religion. Actually, it's the world's most common religion—the religion of egocentricity. So there you are, all alone, this little self that is separate from everything else in the universe. But you are you, with all your ideas and opinions and judgments intact.

In case you are ready to explore this further, I would like to invite you to join us in California this summer for the annual Zen-Catholic retreat. You might find it helpful to be in the company of some very interesting and open religious people, a group of nuns who enrich their own contemplative practice with Zen meditation.

Finding the love beneath the words

CHERI: I enjoy having discussions with people of any religion when I sense they are really having the experience. If they are, they're happy, they're excited, they're growing, they're enthusiastic. Like the preachers you hear on the radio—I love to listen to them while I'm driving. They're just so wound up about the whole thing, and I can enjoy the stew out of that, without caring anything about the content of it.

ELIZABETH: With what attitude of mind do you listen to preachers on the radio?

CHERI: I have no conflict at all with Christianity. Loving one another, accepting one another, opening your heart, the teachings of Jesus—I have no difficulty with that. Now, if someone asks, "Do you believe that you must accept the Lord Jesus Christ as your personal savior?" I would say no, I don't believe that. But it doesn't trouble me that they do.

GENE: I guess I tend to equate a religion with the way some people practice it. If I don't approve of how they practice it, whether it's the Inquisition or conversion by the sword or whatever, I'll think that it's a bad religion, because look what people do in its name.

CHERI: People have done terrible things in the name of religion forever. Should we throw out Zen because we hear that at a Zen center people are doing something we decide is wrong? I hope not.

When I was a child, a "born-again" Christian fellow said to me in this heated discussion we were having, "If you let a hypocrite come between you and God, that hypocrite is closer to God than you are." That impressed me.

RODNEY: Many of us probably have misgivings about things in Christianity, but you can extract very easily, in a historical way, the enlightened teachings of Jesus Christ from the dogma and doctrine and creeds that have been added by followers who have come since. And there are so many parallels between the enlightenment of Christ and the enlightenment of the Buddha—compassion, opening the heart to all, reducing attachments—that it's easy to love and admire Christ and his teachings. And it's very confirming to me to see those parallels.

MARY: I have been angry with my brother and sister-in-law for having become "born-again" Christians, but finally I realized that to be angry with them, I had to set aside parts of my own path. I was assuming that there was something wrong with their beliefs and projecting that they thought there was something wrong with my practice. But if I stick with examining my own experience, I notice that we can talk together about religious topics, and I'm beginning to see that we actually share a lot. They were drawn to their religion for exactly the same reasons I was drawn to this. The concepts we hold about each other's religion have nothing to do with our experiences, which aren't all that different.

At one point, I felt compelled to write my brother a long letter about all the ways in which I was right. And I got this letter back that basically said, "I think you're really screwed up, and you're probably going to burn in hell, and we can't accept you. Love, Your Brother." I was very upset, and I thought and thought about it, and finally I realized that it showed a certain amount of effort and thoughtfulness and care in taking the time to write me this letter, and in fact, no matter what he says, he shows by the way he actually lives his life that he accepts me totally.

What you think of as the other person's love is in fact the love in you.

RIC: I've had a similar experience. I was lovers for four years with someone whose family was very Irish Catholic, and his mother strongly disapproved of his being gay and of our relationship and of me. He'd write her a long letter, and she'd write back and enclose his letter on which she'd underlined in red all the sins. But also in those letters was so much love of a mother who wanted what she thought was best for her son. And as he and the family went through the process of his dying, it was the love that we saw. His mother spent so much time and effort thinking about him and about us, and we could choose to see that as very, very loving. In a situation like that, if you shift your focus, you can see that you both have a lot in common: you're both hurting, you care about each other, and you want what's best for each other.

MIRIAM: But with these two belief systems clashing, it seems to me there's no way to really connect.

RIC: You could connect if either person stepped out of their identification with a role and simply said, "I love you, and I hear the love in what you're saying to me."

CHERI: And I would hope that as you do that, you would realize that it is one and the same love. What you think of as the other person's love is in fact the love in you.

It is also good to realize that we come to retreat not to get information or answers, but to have the experience of *being* love. We may call it finding our compassion or turning to our hearts, or we could call it being in the presence of the Divine or All That Is or whatever name we use for that. We come here to have the experience of being with ourselves, getting to know ourselves, and recognizing the goodness of our true nature.

In this way I do most deeply vow to train myself.

THE PRECEPTS CEREMONY:
From doubt and confusion
to liberation of the heart

MIRIAM: Would you elaborate on what it means to accept the precepts as vows?

CHERI: For me, it's simply a public statement of what I'm attempting to do in my life. When people say they're trying to live in this way but don't know if they are ready to take this step, that usually means, "I don't think I've perfected myself to the point of being ready to participate in a ceremony like this." But for me, the precepts speak to where I'm going more than where I am. The precepts are the ideal; they represent the deepest desire of my heart. Along with that comes the actual, which is what I am working on at any given moment. If I waited until I was sure I could keep them, I would still be preparing.

MUFFIN: It strikes me as a problem to take a vow that you don't intend to keep or that you don't entirely accept.

CHERI: I wouldn't take it if that were my attitude. That is very different from saying, "I want to keep this more than anything, and I suspect I won't always be able to."

MUFFIN: Is it kind of like Catholic confession? You try to be something, and then you fail, so you go to confession.

CHERI: Not to me. Rather, you go to *compassion*, which is the beginning and ending point of spiritual practice.

GREG: If I say this is what it means to keep the precepts, and I can't do it, then I am assuming that I know what they mean. Instead, there can be a sense of not knowing what's possible and doing the best I can according to what my understanding is now. It's just like meditation: I don't know if the experience I have in meditation now is all there is, but that's the experience I'm having now. There's no reason to decide that this must be all there is, therefore I should always have this kind of experience, or that this isn't it and I must be doing something wrong.

CHERI: What Greg is describing is my experience of humility. Doing the best I can right now, not assuming it's the best anybody can do or even the best I might do at some other time, but accepting that this is my best now, while keeping my heart and mind open to the possibility that there's something more.

ELIZABETH: Taking vows sounds a bit like joining a church.

CHERI: It is. You get these beads and this emblem of a key to wear around your neck and things like that. The beads are a rosary we use when we recite the Daily Recollection.

GENE: When you go back to your regular life, do you have to wear the beads all the time?

CHERI: I'm not going to follow you around and find out. So you're going to be left with that decision.

DENNIS: You wear them unless you're going to break a precept. [laughter]

CHERI: I wear mine all the time. I think of it this way: the key reminds me of willingness, and I don't want to be anywhere without willingness.

Before eating, I always bow and say to myself, "As I fill my body with nourishment, so may I fill my mind with love, wisdom, and compassion." I know all the monks say something, and I guess they say the same thing. But at the Zen Center I hear that people are embarrassed to do that. They like saying it, but if there's anybody else around or they're in a restaurant, they won't do it. And I confess, I was astounded, because that never occurred to me. In the same way, it never occurred to me that I wouldn't want to wear the beads that I received when I took the precepts. So I'm not a good one to ask.

But if I had doubts about taking the precepts, I probably wouldn't do it. I often tell people, "Don't start spiritual practice until you can't help yourself." Don't do it because you should or because all your friends are doing it or it might be an interesting experience to have. Each one of you has to make your own decision about it.

As far as I'm concerned, there's no reason to do anything or not do anything. Taking the precepts is like living with someone and then deciding to get married. It may not change anything, it may change all kinds of things. It's simply acknowledging what you are already doing. If you live with somebody and you feel committed to one another and you really care about one another, there's no reason you can't live together for the rest of your lives and be perfectly happy. But sometimes there's just something in people that makes them want to go ahead and get married, to make that sort of statement in the world. For myself, I know it would be much easier for me to walk away from a relationship when there's nothing binding. In the heat of the moment, if I'm sick of you and there's nothing keeping me here, I can just put all my stuff in the car, and I'm gone. But if I have made this commitment, it's a little more complex than that. What I've agreed to in that commitment is to stop and think about it. To look at it more deeply. To accept things in this relationship that I might not accept in other relationships.

DENNIS: I do see it as a marriage—a marriage to a particular piece of myself, to something within me, an affirmation that that's what is important in my life. So, the ceremony was a major step for me as a public affirmation. But actually working with the precepts is what it is really all about. My marriage is the same: the ceremony was very important, but the meaning of the vows I took—that is the true marriage. I feel the same about this, going through a precepts retreat for the second time.

GREG: For me, the public statement makes it more difficult to give up on myself. It's like wanting to stop smoking. I could privately make the decision to stop smoking, but if I really want to, the best way is to tell everybody. The public statement is a way of making myself a little more accountable, making it less likely that I'll believe the first voice that says, "I can't do it, this is too hard." This is almost using egocentricity to help dissolve egocentricity, because part of me doesn't want other people to know I didn't stick it out with what I said I was going to do.

GENE: It seems to me that these precepts are tools we can use to examine our behavior in everything we do. We could create exceptions for all of them, like, I won't tell lies unless it's to keep from hurting somebody's feelings. You could find a similar condition for every one of them, but that removes you from having to examine your behavior. I accept that whether I take these precepts or not, I'm going to break them. There's no doubt about that. Probably as soon as I leave here . . .

RIC: Maybe sooner.

CHERI: Even during the ceremony!

GENE: . . . but the whole idea is that this gets me to examine, and as I continue through my life, maybe change will arise from the examination. It's not to make myself feel guilty, or through any act of will to make myself be better. But if you weaken these tools, you remove yourself from situations where you have a chance look at what you're doing.

CHERI: If we use these against ourselves so that if we keep them we're good and if we don't keep them we're bad, then we do need to weaken them, because who wants to get up every day and feel like a bad person? Instead, we're looking at it from the point of view of, "This is going to help me, this is the strongest magnifying glass I can find with which to scrutinize every behavior." If you're going to move closer to keeping these precepts, the one thing you'll be required to give up is indulging in punishing yourself. When we sincerely begin to examine these kinds of things, we quickly realize that beating ourselves up is not helpful. In fact, it's the biggest stumbling block in living our lives the way we want to live them.

KAREN: I attended a retreat at the monastery not knowing it was a precepts retreat. I went through feeling, "I didn't sign up for this, and I don't want to do it," and seeing the precepts as rules that I couldn't live up to, and seeing some parts of my life that seemed in such direct conflict with the precepts that I could not possibly accept them as vows. It took me up to the last minute to decide whether I was going to do the ceremony or not.

Looking back, I think there was something inside me saying that that was the right time. The process of considering all these things, just as we're doing here, and then going through the ceremony seems like one of the most important things I've ever done for myself. It felt like a commitment to my heart. It was the first time I was aware that I had a moral place inside me from which I could decide things. That is profound to me, to feel that sense of rightness coming from inside.

It was interesting to see how all this played itself out in my life. I didn't know how it would be, going back to things

I'd done before, which I'd never questioned. Some of them just dropped away, because my relationship to them became totally different. Others are still issues for me. The process continues to evolve in response to whatever comes up in my life, and something seems to keep me oriented as I go along.

CHERI: There's almost the sense that your heart has been kept in bondage, and that something about taking the precepts liberates your heart. That's an aspect of it we don't often look at; we only see that these are going to be restrictions on our ego. But there's that deeper part of us that's been held captive by the demands of egocentricity and is liberated in this process.

ELLEN: I've been considering an aspect of taking the precepts that seems related to sangha [the community of those following this path]. I was fairly sure I wanted to take the precepts six months ago. I don't know what it will be like afterwards, but I imagine the commitment as having to do with stepping out of myself into another realm of selves. I don't know any other way to say it. Does that make sense?

CHERI: It does to me. Your effort strengthens the efforts of others, and their efforts strengthen you. That is the beauty and wonder of sangha. I might not show up for myself, but I will show up if others are counting on me. And I know they're showing up to support me.

I have the opportunity to be with people in a way that hardly anybody has. Other relationships in people's lives can be close and intimate, but the one of people seeking guidance in spiritual practice is unique, I think. In that act, people are so vulnerable, so innocent, so pure. And sangha—one hopes, one wishes—is a place where that can be experienced. So when we see someone doing something we think is not right, what we refer to is the innocence of their being, not their action.

We work toward purifying, if you will, that which is harmful by allowing those things within us to arise and by bringing them into this place of clarity to be embraced, to be healed, and then to fall away. We realize that we've spent lifetimes clinging to those things, avoiding them, trying to hide them. To have a safe place where people can be who they are, including the worst that they are, and still be accepted with the acknowledgement that they are doing very, very hard work that no one else can understand—that is very precious.

MARY ELLEN: These precepts can seem scary to me until I put them in the context of the Daily Recollection, where at the end of every section it says, "In this way I do most deeply vow to train myself." When I'm being hard on myself for not doing as well as I think I should, that's the reminder to me that I'm not doing this because I'm already there; rather, I'm in a process.

CHERI: I remember when Jan had an awareness about playing the piano—how you love to practice the piano because you're just practicing and it's fun and you can try new things and really enjoy it, as compared to a performance, where every muscle is tense, the pressure is on, you're terrified of making a mistake, and it's not fun at all. It's good to keep in mind that what we're doing is a practice, not a performance. What we're doing is spiritual training.

JOHN: The analogy about taking the precepts being like getting married—does that extend to something like last-minute cold feet? I didn't have any doubts at all when I came to this retreat—up until about maybe an hour ago.

CHERI: All of the forces come up in the final hour. It's the cold feet of the pre-precepts discussions.

Hi, I'm a Buddhist

RODNEY: My mind has been working with the consequences in my life of taking the precepts and particularly the prospect of wearing a necklace of beads in northwest Florida . . .

GENE: Known as the "Redneck Riviera."

RODNEY: I expect I'll be taking them off about Brewton, Alabama. I've been thinking about the recommendation to "seek not enlightenment, but cease to cherish opinions." This may be the acid test of turning my back on the opinion of others who are going to make it most uncomfortable for me to wear those beads.

GREG: You could always get California license plates for your car. That would explain it.

CHERI: You may not actually want to wear the beads on every occasion. It's not a contest. There's nothing to prove.

Let's say I don't like the idea of letting other people's opinion—which, of course, is my opinion projected onto other people—dictate how I live. Remember how Peter denied Jesus three times? When it was predicted that he would do that, Peter was horrified: "No, absolutely not, I would never do that." But he did; he wasn't able to stand up for what he felt so strongly about. That's a difficult teaching to receive. It would be easy to judge Peter in that situation, but I don't want to because I know that experience in myself.

We can look at that tendency in the same way that we're looking at all of these other things: where does that come from in me? What do I believe about that? What do I feel about it? Rather than, "I'm going to put on these beads and walk right into that family reunion, and nobody is going to stop me." With that attitude, you might want to ask yourself, why am I so eager to set myself up for that kind of suffering?

GENE: To me, it's not so much whether people will approve of what I'm doing. It's that spirituality has always been private to me, and I anticipate that having this external symbol will make people curious. I'll have to try to explain, and that prospect makes me self-conscious.

CHERI: And in that situation—because that will arise—I encourage you to offer way less than it seems people are asking for.

RIC: There's a cynic in me thinking that wearing something around my neck and speaking up for vegetarianism come dangerously close to attachment to a certain identity. It's like having a religious bumper sticker on your car, or wearing a card saying, "Hi, I am so-and-so"—like a label proclaiming who I am.

CHERI: Instead of the labels you're usually attached to?

RIC: I thought we were pretending it was otherwise.

ELLEN: Is this what you're thinking, Ric? That there is a contradiction in striving to end our suffering by nonattachment, and then attaching ourselves to a label or a symbol?

RIC: Yes. I love ceremonies, and yet another side of me thinks a ceremony is another way of clinging. I don't want to convey the message, "Look at me, I'm into Zen." One voice is telling me how nice it would be to wear those beads around my neck, while another voice is skeptical about it.

GREG: We spend our whole lives listening to voices telling us how awful we are, and when one says, "Gee, I'd like to meditate," we say, "What? You're trying to make yourself better than everyone?" If you believe that voice, you could never do anything to end your suffering, because it will always tell you that whatever it is, you're just trying to make yourself big.

ELLEN: I've also found egocentricity getting its hooks in by saying, "Well, you just want to be part of a club." My partner and some of my close friends have taken the precepts, and that's a factor for me, so I can see the same experience from two different places.

CHERI: If you were doing this for the motivation of just wanting to belong to the club, the voices of egocentricity would never bring that up. So I would encourage you to consider whether that's a response to your sincerity, not to insincerity. Try saying, "Yeah, I really do want to join a club." And then the voice says, "You just want to be better than everybody else." And you say, "Yes, I do." Then egocentricity will bring up the next thing, and again the answer is, "Yes. You're right." Just try it and see what happens.

Ten thousand things against us, minus one

KAREN: Sometimes the feeling that I understand this intellectually helps me let go and be centered. Is that possible?

CHERI: It seems to be. You could all just come in and sit on your cushions and look at the wall for several years, and when somebody steps on a creaky board, suddenly you're enlightened, all your questions are answered, and that would be the end of it, just like in the old stories. However, this is America, and it doesn't usually happen that way.

KAREN: It fascinates me that there's some part of me that senses the intrinsic truth in things, and that helps me to be more present.

CHERI: Absolutely. We can be sitting here, and there's a little moment of clarity, and we think, "Oh, yes, okay, I can see that." Then the voices start in again, but we bring our attention back, and there's a little moment of clarity. We're closing in on that clarity all the time. At first there are ten thousand things against it and not one thing for it that we know of. But when we begin to have our own experience of that clarity or intrinsic purity or inherent goodness, there are ten thousand things against it, minus one. And then minus two, and then minus three. It's like a mortgage payment—at some point we're paying on the principal and not the interest.

In this practice of looking inward, if we haven't reached our own goodness, we haven't gone far enough. But the moment we stop doing everything else, goodness is what is there.

In this way I do most deeply vow to train myself.

The precepts ceremony began and ended in the meditation hall. In between was a lengthy period of walking meditation outdoors: a line of people with folded hands following the teacher in her black robe, one slow step at a time. In the silence of pebbled paths covered with damp leaves, we moved through a cold, heavy mist. As we approached the meditation hall, the mist dispersed and a shaft of sunlight fell on the path ahead, and then on us.

Fifteen people accepted the precepts, along with Buddhist refuge vows, in the formal ceremony. After six years, most of them continue to practice meditation and attend Zen retreats, where most (but not all) wear their beads.

DAILY RECOLLECTION

Dharma bead

Dharma is the teaching, the understanding, the contents of the enlightened mind. It is the experience of the joy of intelligence knowing itself.

1st bead: The blessings of love and respect we offer to all, in times past and present, who have opened the doors of wisdom, reuniting all beings with their intrinsic purity.

Marker: ***In this way I do most deeply vow to train myself.***

2nd bead: The recitation of this Rosary ever expands the awakening of faith in the Three Jewels: Bodhi, Dharma, and Sangha.

3rd bead: Bodhi saranam gacchami, dutiyampi, tatiyampi savaha. I turn to the Perfect Nature of Truth for guidance, again and yet again, may it be so.

4th bead: Dharmam saranam gacchami, dutiyampi, tatiyampi savaha. I turn to the Teachings for guidance, again and yet again, may it be so.

5th bead: Sangham saranam gacchami, dutiyampi, tatiyampi savaha. I turn to the Holy Order for guidance, again and yet again, may it be so.

Marker: ***In this way I do most deeply vow to train myself.***

6th bead: Dukkha, the Noble Truth of suffering.

7th bead: Dukkha Samudaya, the Noble Truth of the origin of suffering.

8th bead: Dukkha Nirodha, the Noble Truth of the extinction of suffering.

9th bead: Dukkha Nirodha Gamini Patipada, the Noble Truth of the path that leads to the extinction of suffering.

10th bead: So long as these Four Noble Truths are not understood, we shall wander in sorrow and ignorance.

Marker: *In this way I do most deeply vow to train myself.*

11th bead: All formations are transient—Anicca.

12th bead: All formations are subject to suffering—Dukkha.

13th bead: All things are without a self—Anatta.

Marker: *In this way I do most deeply vow to train myself.*

14th bead: Namo Prajna Paramita Hridaya. Homage to the wisdom in the heart.

15th bead: Form is not different from emptiness, emptiness is not different from form. This is the teaching of our spiritual ancestors, Gotama Buddha, and all the great teachers who have transmitted the Dharma to this holy day.

16th bead: Blessed is the knowledge of emptiness.

17th bead: Homage to the devotees of this and all paths of self-purification. May all find simplicity the joyous and practical guide.

18th bead: The Dharma, being the contents of enlightenment, in which there is no bondage and no suffering, offers freedom from the cankers of ignorance and fear.

Marker: *In this way I do most deeply vow to train myself.*

Sangha bead

Sangha is the Holy Order of spiritual ancestors, monks, priests, and all those who follow and practice this path.

19th bead: Homage to the Sangha.

20th bead: Homage to all who are approaching this Holy Path.

21st bead: Homage to all who follow and establish this Holy Path.

Marker: **In this way I do most deeply vow to train myself.**

22nd bead: By right comprehension that dissipates delusion.

23rd bead: By right aspiration that harms no one.

24th bead: By right speech that makes for clarity.

25th bead: By right self-discipline that brings no regret.

26th bead: By right livelihood that brings no discredit.

27th bead: By right endeavor that results in goodness.

28th bead: By right mindfulness that proves this Path.

29th bead: By right awareness that leads to Nirvana.

Marker: **In this way I do most deeply vow to train myself.**

30th bead: With this recitation I do confirm my acceptance of these three pure precepts.

31st bead: The precept of restraint and religious observances.

32nd bead: The precept of obedience to all good laws.

33rd bead: The precept to benefit all sentient beings.

Marker: **In this way I do most deeply vow to train myself.**

34th bead: With this recitation I do confirm my acceptance of these ten grave prohibitive precepts.

35th bead: Not to lead a harmful life, nor to encourage others to do so (not to kill).

36th bead: Not to take that which is not given (not to steal).

37th bead: Not to commit or participate in unchaste conduct (not to covet).

38th bead: Not to tell lies nor practice believing the fantasies of authority (not to say that which is untrue).

39th bead: Not to use intoxicating drinks or narcotics nor assist others to do so (not to sell the wine of delusion).

40th bead: Not to publish other people's faults (not to speak against others).

41st bead: Not to extol oneself and slander others (not to be proud of oneself and devalue others).

42nd bead: Not to be avaricious in bestowal of the teachings (not to be mean in giving either Dharma or wealth).

43rd bead: Not to be angry.

44th bead: Not to speak ill of this religion or any other (not to defame the three treasures).

Marker: **In this way I do most deeply vow to train myself.**

45th bead: In the practice of loving kindness.

46th bead: In the practice of pure attention.

47th bead: In the practice of ever-expanding faith.

48th bead: In the practice of constant devotion.

49th bead: In the practice of inquiry through correct dhyana.

Marker: **In this way I do most deeply vow to train myself.**

50th bead: Oh, happy Blessed Day.

51st bead: Oh, happy Blessed Place.

52nd bead: Oh, happy Blessed Time.

53rd bead: Oh, happy Blessed Path.

54th bead: Oh, happy Blessed Opportunity.

Marker: **In this way I do most deeply vow to train myself.**

55th bead: Here in humble submission, in order to experience this most perfect now, I deeply bow and sacrifice all thoughts, all tensions, all pressures and desires.

Bodhi bead

I am born of karma, I am heir to karma, I abide in karma, and I am supported by karma. Whatever I do creates karma, and I shall surely experience this karma. The merit for all good acts I do freely offer to all beings. Dutiyampi, tatiyampi, savaha—again and yet again, may it be so.

The Key

Willingness is the name of the key to the gate of awakening, for even to awaken from deep sleep and face the new day, there must be willingness to do it. Here in my hand is the opportunity, and the way is clear beyond the gate of thought and desire. There is no self and other as the awareness of pure undisturbed consciousness slips into all consciousness.

Copy editing and editorial/marketing consulting
    Articulate INK, Sylva, North Carolina

Design and cover
    The Design Den, Denver, Colorado

Photographs
    Mary Ellen Hammond

Art consultant
    Leah Friedman